85

D1281514

Questions Jesus Raised

To
Mepkin Abbey
in
Thanksgiving
by
The Rev. Donald McPhail

DOP
225.786
L07
c2

QUESTIONS JESUS RAISED

ROGER LOVETTE

BROADMAN PRESS
Nashville, Tennessee

MEPKIN ABBEY
1098 Mepkin Abbey Road
Moncks Corner, S.C. 29461

© Copyright 1986 • Broadman Press
All Rights Reserved
4222-59
ISBN: 0-8054-2259-5
Dewey Decimal Classification: 226.5
Subject Heading: BIBLE N.T. JOHN—SERMONS
Library of Congress Catalog Number: (to come)
Printed in the United States of America

Unless otherwise stated, all Scripture quotations are from the Revised Standard Version of the Bible, copyrighted 1946, 1952, © 1971, 1973.
Scripture quotations marked GNB are from the *Good News Bible*, the Bible in Today's English Version. Old Testament: Copyright © American Bible Society 1976; New Testament copyright © American Bible Society 1966, 1971, 1976. Used by permission.
Scripture quotations marked ASV are from the American Standard Version of the Bible.

Library of Congress Cataloging in Publication Data

Lovette, Roger, 1935-
    Questions Jesus raised.

    1. Bible. N.T. John—Sermons.   2. Baptists—
Sermons.   3. Southern Baptist Convention—Sermons.
4. Sermons, American.   I. Title.
BS2615.4.L68   1985   226'.506   85-15137
ISBN 0-8054-2259-5 (pbk.)

For my mother

Contents

Contents

Introduction

Years ago, in a seminary preaching class, each student had to deliver a sermon to fellow class members. One day a young man, anxious to please, stood up before the professor and his peers to give his first sermon. Pale and nervous, he began the sermon by dramatically looking at his watch and asking: "What time is it?" Some wag in the back of the class responded: "It's 2:25." That brought down the house and broke the tension. Some questions are not meant to be answered.

The Book of John contains no hypothetical questions. There are more than twenty questions that Jesus raised in the Fourth Gospel. Each question demanded a response.

Our age is suspicious of questions, but craves answers desperately. Our best-sellers tell us how to fix love, marriage, and divorce, how to shed forty pounds, make money, and which color makes us beautiful. In desperation, we gobble up these instant cures and wonder why so little changes.

Jesus gave no easy answers in John's Gospel, but He did ask some hard questions. In this book we will study the major questions that Jesus asked. He directed them toward a great many different people. Saints and sinners, and all those in between, were forced to live with the questions Jesus raised.

Recently, I read of a little boy named Michael who loved the stories his parents read to him. He loved them so much he decided he would climb into a book. He did not believe so wonderful a world was unreachable; he simply opened the book of his favorite story, carefully placed the book on the floor, and stepped in. He tried again and again, certain he would get it right. Each time he was left standing on the book, crying in bewilderment.[1]

Christians believe we can step into the story. Thomas wears our face. Peter is our brother. Mary asks our question, and the church is sometimes as callous as the crowd Jesus faced. As we climb into the story and let their questions become ours, the Gospel comes alive. He speaks our names. Like Lazarus, He calls us forth. We are never the same again.

Preachers may discover here some ideas for Sunday. Laypeople may see this splendid Gospel in a different way. Students who find faith hard may receive some encouragement in these pages. Some would-be disciple like Nathanael or Nicodemus may come upon a door opening.

This book would have never been written without my own church that first allowed me to raise these questions in sermon form and, then, generously gave me a month off to finish this project. No pastor has a finer congregation to serve than the First Baptist Church in Clemson, South Carolina. I thank them all. But I also thank Dr. Robert Hill who challenged my presuppositions and helped with the revisions; my secretary, Jean Thomas, who took so much of her own time to type this manuscript; Sanford Beckett and Jeff Hobart, my colleagues, who worked so hard while I was away writing; but my deepest thanks go to my wife, Gayle who read, encouraged, and stood by me always.

If, in reading these questions, you deal with your own questions and God's answers—then this book will have been worth the effort.

Roger Lovette

Note

1. Carol Sternhell, "Bellow's Typewriters and Other Tics of the Trade," *The New York Times Book Review,* 2 Sept. 1984, p. 1.

1
The Conversion Question:
John 1:35-42

> He comes to us as One unknown, without a name, as of old, by the lake-side, He came to those men who knew Him not. He speaks to us the same word: "Follow thou me!" and sets us to the tasks which He has to fulfil for our time. He commands. And to those who obey Him, whether they be wise or simple, He will reveal Himself in the toils, the conflicts, the sufferings which they shall pass through in His fellowship, and, as an ineffable mystery, they shall learn in their own experience Who He is.[1]
>
> —Albert Schweitzer

The Gospel of John begins the ministry of Jesus with a question. Most important things start with a question. Early in Genesis, the garden rang with God's terrible words: "Where are you?" (Gen. 3:9). Later, in that same book, Cain would reckon with his brother's murder as God asked, "Where is Abel your brother?" (4:9). Moses and Isaiah began their ministries in response to a question. Elijah in his depression, Jeremiah with fire in his bones, Amos surrounded by a callous people—all fell victim to questions that changed their lives.

The questions continue in the New Testament. There are more than twenty-one questions that Jesus

12

asks in John's Gospel alone. Afterwards, Saul would turn Paul when God asked, "Saul, Saul, why persecutest thou me?" (Acts 9:4). Substract the questions from the Scriptures, and the Book would be poorer indeed. The questions are everywhere.

Where would we be without our questions? We ask: Will you marry me? What will I do with my life? How much does the job pay? Is it a boy or a girl? Is there a malignancy? How long does she have? Like those hinge-turning questions in the Bible, many of our questions determine the doors we open and the rooms where we will spend our lives.

Jesus' first question began with conversion. He asked Andrew and his friend: "What are you looking for?" (John 1:38, GNB). He challenged them to look at their priorities, what they wanted out of life, what, more than anything else, they had been looking for all their days.

But Jesus caught them off guard. They could not answer that question at first. Either they misunderstood what he asked, or they did not expect so direct a question. They responded foolishly: "Where are you staying?" They really did not answer Jesus at all. Instead, they asked where He lived, what town He came from, what His address was. Their response was superficial.

Jesus threw those two a challenge. It was the same call that Adam and Moses and Elijah and all the rest had heard down through the years. "Come and see," He said (v. 39). He invited them to discover for themselves.

What a discovery it was to be—water turned to wine, men sick all their lives made well and whole, prostitutes forgiven and changed, thousands fed on a hillside! On and on it would go until Andrew and the others would

understand. Deep in their hearts they would know who
He was and what He really did.

All important journeys must deal with the conversion
question. What are we looking for? Our age can certainly answer such a question. We want to take ten pounds
off. We want to dress right for success. We want to
climb the ladder and get ahead. We want to know how
to prosper in the coming bad years. We want to win by
intimidation, look out for number one, and have more
joy in sex. Millions of us answer daily with responses as
superficial as those first hearers.

Jesus does not walk away from the twentieth century
and leave us with our emptiness. The same challenge
that rang out in Galilee still comes to us: "Come and
see."

The conversion question, more than anything else, is
a voyage of discovery. He invites us, as He invited those
long ago, to come and see for ourselves.

In John that theme of discovery would be worked out
over and over as the pages turn and the story unfolds
until, toward the end, the author added with a flourish:
"These are written that you may believe that Jesus is
the Christ, the Son of God, and that believing you may
have life in his name" (20:31).

Those first followers found far more than where He
stayed. They found life everlasting. Their water was
turned to wine. Their brokenness found a mending.
Their sins were forgiven. Their hungers were met and
filled forever. Jesus would change it all.

In response to Jesus' question, Andrew and his friend
had asked, "Where are you staying?" This word stay can
also be translated "abide." *Abide* is an important word
in John's Gospel (ASV) to describe a reciprocal partici-

pation of our life in another. John used this word three times in this story. Where do you *abide* (v. 38, ASV)? They went and saw where he was *abiding* (v. 39, ASV). They *abode* with Him all day long (v. 39, ASV). Ever so tentatively, they began to participate in His life, and they found their own hearts unalterably changed.

Faith still comes when we abide with Him. If we, like Andrew and the others, open our lives to a relationship with Christ, we will come to know Him too. As we learn to pray, discover the quiet times, lift our hearts in worship, and engage in meaningful service we will begin to understand the meaning of this word *abide*.

One preacher tells of a character in a short story who had committed terrible sins against his wife. In desperation, she finally divorced him. Years later she met him, and her anger boiled to the surface again. She remembered the pain and heartache he had caused. Now the man was married again and a respectable member of the community. She wanted to expose the hypocrisy of her former husband for all to see. She wanted him to hurt as she had been hurt. She challenged him to take off the mask he had worn all those years. Let them all see, she said, what you really look like. Slowly, the man peeled away the mask. The woman was amazed. He had become, through the years, the mask he wore. As we begin to abide in Christ, our lives will be changed, too.

John's first story was not over. Andrew ran and called his brother, Simon. He told him about this newfound friend. And Simon came to discover for himself what the others had found.

Slowly, the conversion question changed their lives. Years later, they would remember a day years before when the sun was high in the sky. The time was about four o'clock in the afternoon. There stood One who asked them an ultimate question. It was a question that forced them to deal with what they really wanted out of life, a question about coming, seeing, and following. That shining day they made their response. They would always remember, and they would be glad. The memory never faded, and the feeling never changed.

Note

1. Albert Schweitzer, *The Quest of the Historical Jesus*, trans. W. Montgomery (New York: Macmillan, 1968), p. 403.

2
The Faith Question:
John 1:45-51

Thomas a Kempis once recorded a soliloquy in the quiet of his heart which began with a fearful survey of the future. "Oh," he mused, "if only I knew I would hold out to the last." And his soul rose up and answered him with scorn. "Look back," it cried, "Has God ever failed you in the past?" "No." "And don't you know," the voice said, "that the same God who has been, and who is so evidently sufficient, will be with you every step to the end, always as gloriously present for you then as now?"

As we move through the first chapter of John's Gospel, we see the circle of discipleship widening. First, there was John the Baptist pointing to Jesus and saying, "Behold, the Lamb of God!" (v. 36). Then Andrew and his friend came, heard, and followed. Andrew ran and corralled his brother, Simon. Moving north the next day toward Galilee, Jesus found Philip. And Philip, excited and breathless, ran to tell his friend Nathanael.

"We have found the Messiah," Philip said. "We have found him of whom Moses in the law and also the prophets wrote, Jesus of Nazareth, the son of Joseph." But Nathanael wondered: "Can any thing good come out of Nazareth?" (v. 46). But Philip was persistent. He used the words that Jesus, Himself, had used the day before: "Come and see."

Reluctantly, Nathanael came and saw more than he intended. Suddenly, Nathanael encountered Jesus firsthand. Jesus spoke before the man could think of a thing to say. "Behold, an Israelite indeed, in whom is no guile!" (v. 48). Nathanael was impressed with more than the flattery. He had heard all those things before. He was moved because Jesus knew him through and through. Only a prophet could have known how he sat, hours on end, reading the Law under a fig tree. Only someone very special could have known his name even though they had never met. Nathanael was impressed by Jesus' knowledge of him. He exclaimed: "Rabbi, you are the Son of God! You are the King of Israel!" (v. 49).

But all this was background. These words merely form the framework for the second question Jesus would ask in John's Gospel. This query is a question of belief. Jesus asked Nathanael, "Because I said to you, I saw you under the fig tree, do you believe?" (v. 50).

This second question was a faith question: Why do you believe? These words were not only addressed to some first-century would-be disciple, they were addressed to all of us who walk across the stage. "Tell Me honestly," Jesus said, "why do you believe?"

John does not give us Nathanael's reply. But we have all answered this faith question. We believe because we were brought up this way. We got up on Monday morning, ate our breakfast, and went off to school. We got up on Sunday morning and went to church.

Sometimes we say we believe because one dark night we had gone about as far as we could go. We didn't know what to say or do. And we found ourselves doing something we never did very often except in a pinch. We prayed. We got down on our knees and prayed and prayed. And, somehow, it happened. And that's why we believe.

Some of us believe because we think the teachings of the church are good for our families. The family that prays together stays together. It certainly won't hurt. It may just help. And that's why we believe.

Nathanael believed because before him stood One that knew his name before they had ever been introduced. He was impressed because Jesus knew his past history. Here was someone who could read the signs in the heavens and maybe even in a person's heart. Anybody would believe someone who knew so much.

But Nathanael's faith was tentative and fragile. This was the faith that sees a miracle and believes. This is elementary first-grade trust. He was dazzled by a miracle and responded. This believing reminds me of people who pray for God to give them every silly wish. If we see, we will believe.

We know this kind of faith well. Give us a sign. Heal our child. Mend our marriage. Send us a job. Get me out of the mess I'm in. Take away the pain.

There is a faith that demands physical results. John says that Nathanael saw someone who knew much about him, so he believed. Some days, it was easy to believe.

But Jesus was not impressed with the confession of Nathanael. He knew this man had a long way to go: Do you believe because I said I saw you under a fig tree? Then Jesus followed His question with a promise, "Truly, truly, I say to you, you will see heaven opened, and the angels of God ascending and descending upon

the Son of man" (v. 51). Nathanael, there is another
kind of faith. Another way of seeing. There is a faith
that you know little about. Elementary, first-grade faith
must have a sign, a proof, something nailed down and
proven. There is a test-tube faith that can be measured
and analyzed. But there is another kind of faith. This
deeper kind of faith is also seeing. But this seeing is so
strange and different that it takes a lifetime to know.
"You will see heaven opened, and the angels of God
ascending and descending upon the Son of man." Jesus
told Nathanael there was a seeing that he had yet to
discover.

The disciple Thomas knew the first kind of faith. He
had known it most of his life. "Unless I see in his hands
the print of the nails, . . . I will not believe" (John 20:25).
Jesus unfolded the nail-scarred hands and then told
Thomas of a deeper faith, "Blessed are those *who have
not seen* and yet believe" (v. 29, author's italics).

What can we learn about this second kind of faith?
What can we learn about this through-a-glass-darkly
kind of faith that Paul talked of? Faith is sight. Jesus said
this twice in this passage. But this second stage of faith
is not the kind of belief that responds to miracles, to
stab wounds, to signs, or answered prayers. This faith
sight goes far beyond our usual seeing or feeling. This
faith is as strange as angels "ascending and descending
upon the Son of man." This belief is a seeing that most
people never even glimpse in all their lives.

Martin Luther said there are two kinds of believing.
One kind of belief is to believe things about God. He
said there are some things that we can affirm about God
that we can also say about the Turks, the devil, or hell.
These are facts: encyclopedia knowledge. This is belief.

Luther then talked of another kind of faith. Not only do we believe in God, but we begin to put our trust in Him. We bet our lives on the truth that there is a God. We even begin to give Him our money because we really do believe this business. We surrender to Him. We follow Him. We believe that He is with us, and nothing can separate us from His love.

In such a faith relationship we begin to know by experience—to see. But this is a different kind of sight. Here we find a deep, gut-level kind of knowing that no one can take from us. John called this seeing as strange as watching angels ascend and descend upon the Son of man.

Here is one way I have encountered this second kind of faith. On the back wall of a church building where I once served hung an oil painting. I wondered about that painting, and one day someone explained the picture and its history. I was told that a young graduate student and his wife had come to our town. While they were there, they had lost a little girl. They were devastated. They did not know where to turn. They had attended the little Baptist church near the campus on and off, but they had never been very regular.

When the baby got sick, that church had reached out. They prayed. They visited. They took food. They had loved and cared for this young couple. When the baby died, they had walked with the broken couple through their terrible grief. There were days when the young man and his wife wondered if they would make it. Somehow they had found the grace to go on. The young man finally had finished his degree and moved to another place.

But before he left, he had wanted to leave something

behind for the people who had helped him and his wife. He had painted a picture: a beautiful oil painting. It was a pleasant scene with woods and a natural setting. The person who told me the story asked me to look closely at the picture. Can you see it, he asked? I was puzzled. Keep looking, he said. I kept looking, and suddenly the picture began to change. At the heart of that pleasant scene of trees and sky and waterfall, I could make out the shape of a cross and a man on the cross. Jesus was at the center of it all.

That young man had left behind a gift for the church that had been there when he needed them. He had learned, in that awful moment, of seeing even when the glass is dark and the way seemed so unalterably blurred, that Christ is in it. This is the second kind of seeing.

We find Nathanael's name mentioned only once more in the Gospel accounts. His name appears again in the twentieth chapter of John. He was with Peter and the other disciples. Jesus had been crucified. And though Easter had come and gone, nothing seemed to have made much sense. They were still devastated. So Simon Peter led them all back to what they had known before Jesus came into their lives. They returned to fishing nets, water, boats, and seines. They fished all night and caught nothing. Toward morning with the fog heavy on the lake, they heard a voice they had heard before. They knew who it was.

I have wondered often about that story. As they moved toward shore, did Nathanael remember a promise made years before? Did he remember the promise of a faith he had never known? A faith that saw unlikely things, shining things, unbelievable things? A faith that found the strength to go on, people coming back from the dead—resurrections? A faith that endured even when everything seemed to point in another direction? I wonder if Nathanael remembered, that misty morning, the promise of Jesus: "You will see heaven opened, and the angels of God ascending and descending upon the Son of man" (v. 51). Did he remember? I wonder, things being as they are, if we will remember, too.

3
The Identity Question:
John 2:1-11

The miracles of Jesus were the ordinary works of His
Father, wrought small and swift that we might take
them in.[1]

—George MacDonald

Mary's request was certainly understandable. A good
friend of hers, perhaps a relative, was getting married.
In ancient Palestine, the wedding celebration lasted
seven days. Somewhere around the third or fourth day,
Jesus and His disciples arrived. It could have been that
Jesus and His friends' presence heightened Mary's anxiety. There may have already been more at the party
than the family counted on. Mary came to her son with
a simple request: "They have no wine" (v. 2).

We might call it any bride's mother's nightmare. Her
daughter is getting married. Everything is proceeding
as planned. The preacher doesn't call anyone by the
wrong names. The ushers do nothing mortifying. Her
husband does not say the wrong thing. She doesn't even
cry. After the pictures are made, everybody goes down
to the reception. This is where the nightmare begins.
The mother can't find the wedding cake. The punch is
missing. Nobody knows where the cups are. The ice

machine breaks down, and the finger food is lost. In the dream, the poor mother of the bride stands there hoping her mascara won't run and forcing herself not to run out the door screaming while her husband just stands there smiling. She wakes up with a start. The wedding is two weeks away. It is only a dream.

This was no dream in Cana. The wine had run out. You could not have a wedding in Palestine without wine. Hospitality was a sacred duty in that culture. Even the poorest of families had a week-long celebration when someone was married. The newly married couple went on no honeymoon. They stayed home, and for a week they kept their house open. They wore crowns, dressed in their wedding finery, and were treated as king and queen. Their word was law. In a world where poverty and hard work ruled, this festival of joy was often the supreme moment in the couple's life.[2]

Mary's request to Jesus was her way of attempting to solve the problem. "They have no wine." This became the setting of Jesus' third question: "O woman, what have you to do with me? My hour has not yet come" (v. 4). Jesus' words in the original are not as harsh as they appear in the English translation. "Woman" is not a particularly cold term. This was the same word that Jesus used from the cross when He spoke to His mother: "Woman, behold, your son!" (John 19:26). Although He could be stern, the word *woman* was no callous term. Jesus asked: Why does it concern us that they have no wine? If there was a sharpness, it was when He asked what concern that was to her.

Why did Jesus respond so strongly? Mary and Jesus were operating on two different levels of understanding. Mary wanted Jesus to work a miracle and solve her problem. Jesus had something more important in mind. Let us look closely at these two different points of view.

Mary wanted a miracle. Surely Jesus would answer her request. Her sister's family was in trouble. This was no huge demand. Please do something for the family. Give us a minor miracle. Turn the water into wine.

We can all identify with Mary. Here is trouble, and here is Jesus. Lord, won't You do something? The wine has run short. There is not enough to go around. Like Mary, we see religion as the answer.

The wine still runs short. Sickness or disappointments come. In the middle of the best years of our lives, lightning strikes, and life is forever different. Our reach exceeds our grasp. Consequently, we lose our vision. We wake up one day and find a numbness on the inside. We tire too easily. We get angry over the tiniest things. We discover we have limits; it just about kills us.

Like Mary, we turn to religion for our answers. "Jesus," we pray, "there is no wine." Fix our problem. Give us a minor miracle. Help us save face. Solve our problem, and answer our dilemma.

Some anonymous reader of a local newspaper expressed this view several years ago. A midwestern state was facing a drought. One letter writer composed the following prayer: "O Lord, send us and our dusty neighbors around the world a good soaking rain of about one-and-a-half inches over a fifteen-hour period, at the rate of no more than a tenth of an inch per hour, preferably at night and repeat once a week through April 15, with the exception of three weeks appropriate for spring planting; and thereafter once every two weeks until the soil-moisture deficit has been eliminated, or until the farmers wish it would stop, whichever comes first. Amen." Though the man wrote tongue in cheek, he prayed like Mary. He prayed for a miracle. The wine has run out. Give us what we want. Mary misunderstood Jesus and His power when she saw religion as the answer to her problem.

Jesus responded to her demand with a question. This question pointed to a second level of understanding. This sharp question to His mother means that religion is not to be used for our own purposes, to meet whatever requests we make. Jesus' whole identity is bound up in His response to His mother.

Mary, He said, I was not called to save you from embarrassment or to run your errands. The power of God is not to be spent on saving face or some answering service for our requests.

One night a little girl prayed at bedtime, "Dear God, please make Baltimore the capital of Massachusetts." After she finished, her mother wanted to know why she had prayed such an unusual prayer. The little girl told her that she had put Baltimore down on her test paper at school that day as the capital of Massachusetts. She was afraid she would fail. Her prayer was not answered.

When Jesus comes, He gives us far more than we can imagine. Years ago, in a time of crisis, I went to see an aged physician who had helped many troubled people. I sat down and poured out my troubles. I was desperate. I could not sleep. My work was not going well. I did not know how much longer I could continue. After I poured out my concerns, the old doctor took from his desk a little card. He told me he wanted me to read the printed words everyday. He called the words on that card a prescription. The card contained a mimeographed copy of the twenty-third Psalm. He told me to read the words carefully: "You will find some of the words have been changed."

I read, "The Lord is my Shepherd, *I shall not lack.*" The doctor pointed out that there is a world of difference in God giving us what we want and what we need. He told me that God does not answer all our wants, but He gives us what we need. Those words became a life raft for me in a time of trouble. Those words kept me afloat: "The Lord is my Shepherd, *I shall not lack.*" God gave me what I needed, not necessarily what I wanted.

Jesus followed His rebuke to Mary by turning the water into wine. John called this miracle at Cana the first of seven signs. We must note the word *sign*. Signs are very important in John's Gospel. Dr. Fred Craddock said that these signs were windows.[3]

Through the clear glass of this first sign, we see more than a Worker of miracles. Through this window we see a prelude of all that will come. We see how our Lord will enter into people's troubles and suffice for every difficulty. Through this window we see that His coming is as remarkable as water changed to wine.

John said that the servants were directed to bring six large waterpots. Each of these vessels held between twenty and thirty gallons of water. Jesus produced 180 gallons of wine that day. The wine He brings is more than enough for all the occasions of life. Paul understood this miracle story when he wrote to his troubled friends in Ephesus: "By the power at work within us [he] is able to do far more abundantly than all we ask or think" (Eph. 3:20).

I learned this truth personally a year after I had visited the old doctor that first time. I was making my pastoral rounds at the local hospital. Someone told me that the doctor was a patient upstairs. I went to his room and knocked on the door. There was no answer. I knocked a second time and heard a low voice say: "Come in." I entered a darkened room. My doctor-friend was sitting in a chair with his head down. He could hardly look up. He began to explain that he was very sick, and being a doctor, he did not know if he would make it. He was depressed and very worried about his condition. Before I left, I told him I wanted to give him something. I took from my pocket a piece of paper and wrote him a prescription. I wrote: *"The Lord is my Shepherd, I shall not lack."* I handed the paper to my old friend. He read it and nodded. There were tears in his eyes and mine. I had given him back the good news that he had given me a year before.

The turning of the water to wine is more than the record of a mere miracle. Here we discover the first of seven signs. Jesus produced 180 gallons of wine. Here is enough for all we face. Embedded in John's story, we discover the identity of Jesus. This is the meaning of the third question.

Notes

1. George MacDonald, *An Anthology,* ed. C. S. Lewis (New York: Macmillan, 1947), p. 46.

2. William Barclay, *The Gospel of John,* vol. 1 (Philadelphia: Westminster Press, 1956) p. 82.

3. Fred B. Craddock, *John* (Atlanta: John Knox Press, 1982), p. 26.

MEPKIN ABBEY
1098 Mepkin Abbey Road
Moncks Corner, S.C. 29461

4
The Grace Question:
John 3:1-15

"My grace is sufficient" was the text that eventually, after interminable heart-searching, seemed to hold out a chance of life to him. As often with Bunyan the good image is of being held by loving arms. . . . It was "as if it had arms of grace so wide that it could not only inclose me, but many more besides."[1]

—Monica Furlong,
writing of John
Bunyan's conversion

There is no more intriguing character in John's Gospel than Nicodemus. He was an important man, a well-thought-of member of the Pharisees. Standing there in his long robes, he would have been the fit subject for any painter.

John did not linger very long over Nicodemus's credentials. The Gospel simply says that he came to see Jesus at night. Surely a man of his importance had to be careful. He had a reputation to maintain.

We do not know why Nicodemus came. He must have been troubled, even desperate. We do know that he was in his middle years. More days were behind him than lay ahead. There simply was not enough time left. He may have been troubled about many things: inhumanity between persons, injustice, questions about God, and the hereafter. Perhaps he came because of the emptiness in his own heart. We do know that it took courage for any Pharisee to talk to Jesus—even after dark.

Nicodemus opened his conversation with words of flattery: "Rabbi, we know that you are a teacher come from God; for no one can do these signs that you do, unless God is with him" (v. 2). Jesus' response disarmed him: "Truly, truly, I say to you, unless one is born anew, he cannot see the kingdom of God" (v. 3). Nicodemus might have laughed softly. But it may have been a nervous chuckle that people use when they are disarmed. He was a good man, intent and honest. He wouldn't be standing there in the shadows, facing this teacher whom most of his people despised, unless he were open. He didn't understand Jesus' words. Nicodemus responded: "How can a man be born when he is old?" (v. 4).

The word *how* is used more than once in this story. Nicodemus was a good Jew. Maybe he wanted Jesus to give him some formula, something to do. He may have wanted something else to study or some new discipline. There may have been some new law that he had overlooked. Nicodemus was a doer.

Jesus said the most unlikely thing: "Truly, truly, I say to you, unless one is born of water and the Spirit, he cannot enter the kingdom of God" (v. 5). There is only one way to see the kingdom of God—from above. Nicodemus, it is like birth. What in the world did you have to do with being born? Somebody else did it all: father, mother, midwife. Birth is a gift, and the only thing you can do is reach up and claim the air that comes, the light you see, and the love that surrounds you. It comes from outside—above. God gives it.

Nicodemus asked a hypothetical question and was given a practical answer. Jesus refused to deal with the "how." He stood firm. It comes "from above."

This man of great importance was frankly puzzled. He had come at great risk, after dark, to see Jesus. He had brought with him all the troubled questions of his life. What did he find? No real answers at all. He was given some words about being born anew that were not easy to follow.

How in the world could a fifty-year-old start life over again? His habits were well fixed; his role was highly visible; his responsibilities were sharply defined. Nicodemus had a good idea of his limitations and vulnerabilities. Wasn't that maturity—to look at oneself and know what was really there? Jesus told this important ruler of the Jews that he must change drastically if he was to ever see the kingdom of God.

Nicodemus responded as any Pharisee would. He had been trained in the best tradition of the law. He was a ruler over his own people. He sat with seventy other judges over his nation. For a second time he asked: "How can this be?" (v. 9). There must have been desperation in his second question. What must I do? How?

All this is background for Jesus' next question. "Are you a teacher of Israel, and yet you do not understand this?" (v. 10). John's whole Gospel was a book that attempted to clarify the things that seemed so hopelessly muddled. Andrew and his friend stood looking at Jesus in that first chapter. Jesus asked them what they were looking for and they responded in the most foolish way: "Where are you staying?" (v. 38). Jesus' challenge to

"Come and see" took in much more than those two ever dreamed.

Then came Nathanael, half out of curiosity. In following Jesus, this man discovered a world he had never known.

At the wedding at Cana, Mary wanted the water changed to wine.

Nicodemus, too, discovered far more than he intended. He wanted some list to follow, something to do—his "how" answered in terms he could understand. Jesus forced him to see the far horizon.

Three times, Jesus hammered home the point: You must be born from above. Nicodemus, basic change can occur. It won't happen the way Judaism expects it to happen. It has nothing to do with rules, status, honor, and works. It comes from outside, like birth. It is like the water that washes you clean. It is like the wind of the Spirit that moves across your life—felt but never seen.

Jesus' fourth question is a grace question. Nicodemus knew so many things, but he could not understand the birth from above. That birth was a gift. It could not be worked for nor earned. It could not be taken like an education course or bitter medicine. God gives it. Nathanael had learned that faith is a new way of seeing. Jesus told Nicodemus that faith is a gift from God.

Did Nicodemus understand? Did he ever fully come to terms with the grace question? John's Gospel gives us two hints in his story. In John 7 the Jewish officials gathered to discuss Jesus. They had charged Him with many crimes. They sought to condemn Him. They feared His power. Nicodemus, a respected member of the Sanhedrin, a judge and ruler, rose to his feet. In a voice of authority, he spoke a good word for Jesus. No one, he said, should be judged unless they had been heard first-hand. His peers looked at him as if he had lost his mind. Nicodemus stood firm.

John's last picture of Nicodemus comes toward the end of the Gospel. In John 19, Joseph of Arimathea and Nicodemus came with the sad task of preparing Jesus' body for burial. One of Rembrandt's most famous etchings portrays that scene. The limp, dead body was slowly being taken down from the cross. Joseph of Arimathea stood by in all his finery. In the darkness, further away, with his face lined in sorrow, stood Nicodemus. In his hands he held the linen cloth Jesus' body would be buried in.

The Gospel says that Nicodemus brought to that occasion a mixture of myrrh and aloes. As he slipped that mixture of spices into the folds of the linen garment, I wonder if then he understood. Did the old words come back? *Nicodemus, it comes from above. God does it. You can't do it yourself. It's like being cleansed all over, inside and out. And the wind blows, the wind of power, enabling you to do what you thought you could never do.*

Did Nicodemus, after all those years, finally understand? The honor, success, and responsibility counted for nothing. It was grace after all.

Note

1. Monica Furlong, *Puritan's Progress* (New York: Coward, McCann & Geoghegan, Inc. 1975) p. 67.

5
The Health Question:
John 5:1-9

There is a balm in Gilead to make the wounded whole,
There is a balm in Gilead to heal the sin-sick soul.
—black spiritual

Jesus' fifth question is certainly contemporary. "Do you want to be healed?" (v. 6). When the history of the 1980s is written, it will be recorded that we were a people obsessed with health. Health care costs in the United States will rise from $10 billion in 1950 to an estimated $307.2 billion by 1987.[1] The official guess is that we are now investing around eight percent of the gross national produce on health care. This figure could soon climb to ten or twelve percent.[2]

The longing for health is big business. Television and radio focus continually on our lust for health. Night after night, day after day, we are inundated with advertising, books, and articles that promise to cure all our maladies. We buy millions of aids for constipation, headaches, insomnia and anxiety. Tennis, jogging, aerobics, pumping iron, and good nutrition are proclaimed as the cures for the eighties. We are a nation hooked on health, fitness, and well-being. Vitamins, Lewis Thomas has said, have taken the place of prayer.[3]

No character on John's crowded cast is more familiar than the man by the pool of Bethesda. He had been sick for thirty-eight years. John said it was believed that from time to time an angel would come and trouble the waters of the pool of Bethesda. The first person in those swirling waters after the angel's appearance was healed.

But there was a problem. This crippled man had no one to put him into the healing waters. He had been there so long that family and friends had finally abandoned him. Day after day he lived in hope, but his was a hope deferred. Someone else always pushed in front and got into the water before he did. This man had lived by the healing pool for thirty-eight years.

To this place of suffering, Jesus came with His fifth question: "Do you want to be healed?" Like His questions to Mary and Nicodemus, Jesus continued the same theme as He addressed the cripple man. Their requests were all on one level; as usual, Jesus' answer was more far reaching than they imagined.[4]

What does Jesus' fifth question mean? You have been here for thirty-eight years. You are crippled and live life on the verge, merely existing. You monotonously hope for some miracle that never comes. You must have had a thousand false starts and plunges that came too late. *Do you want to be healed?* Do you want what you say you want? This question was a painful question. Arthur Gossip has pointed out that often the life to which we are accustomed may hold more allurements than the life to which we long.[5]

This fifth question is a question of wants. The matter of the will is primary to all action. *What do you really want?* If our desires, like Mary's and Nicodemus's are

partial and small, then our healings, too, may be inci-
dental and limited. We need more than wine for wed-
dings and answers to our theological questions. We also
need more than shriveled legs made strong. Do we
want to be healed? Do we want a different life than
lying on some pallet on the verge of life.

The proper prayer for any real healing begins here.
Carlyle Marney once said that we are to pray that God
will fix our "wanters." We pray that the deep desires of
our hearts will square with the intentions of God for our
lives.

Any casual reading of advertising today uncovers the
wants of our times. We want better physiques and flat
stomachs, to be successful and more popular. We want
to hold back the wrinkles and the telltale signs of our
humanity. These wants are primarily selfish and small
—distractions from the concerns of life—and in these
small wantings, no healing of consequence will come.
Our wills must square with His—this is our only hope.

When our wants are clearly acknowledged, we begin
to encounter the real challenge behind Jesus' fifth question: "Do you want to be healed?" (v. 6).

Health, like salvation, means wholeness. Health
means that there will flow into all parts of our lives a
wellness. The old gospel song captures the meaning of
this real health: "It is well with my soul."

This wellness is concerned with far more than strong
bodies. This health means to flow outward toward others. There is little wholeness that does not take in brothers, husbands, children, neighbors, and world. Our
current craze of physical well-being seems to ignore all
the larger dimensions of real health. Lewis Thomas
says:

We should be worrying that our preoccupation with
personal health may be a symptom of copping out, an
excuse for running upstairs to recline on a couch,
sniffing the air for contaminants, spraying the room
with deodorants, while just outside, the whole of society
is coming undone.[5]

Healthy people, Jesus said, penetrate a world with
salt and light. They become the keys to the Kingdom
and the leaven in the loaf. They matter at every level
of society. Health that does not move beyond self is
little wholeness at all.

Jesus' words to the lame man were similar to the
words He gave His Mother and Nicodemus. His challenge was much larger than they expected. "Rise, take
up your pallet, and walk" (v. 8).

Christ did not place the man in the troubled waters.
He spoke in the imperative: Get up! Pick up your pallet!
Walk! And the man stood on crippled, skinny legs. They
wobbled. But he stood. He put a trembling hand on a
post for support. He held tightly as he slowly stooped
down. The crowd held their breath. They were sure he
would fall. Slowly and painfully, he picked up his pallet
and put it on his shoulder. Then he straightened up.
With a smile he began to walk away. For the first time
in thirty-eight years, he was going home.

John calls what happened that day a sign. This, too,
is a window through which we see many things. An age
obsessed with lean, rippling bodies sees its wants spread
out before them and judged. We also see underneath
the anguish of our times and the emptiness of our lives
that wholeness comes to those who really ask, seek, and
knock. But we see more through that window. We see
the power of God in Jesus—adequate for whatever we

face. None are immune, and none are left out. We can all be healed.

A century after John penned his Gospel, those who followed Jesus were driven underground by Rome into the catacombs. On the walls of those dark, dark rooms they left behind their last will and testament of what He had done in their lives. Again and again, they drew a picture of a lame man striding away with a pallet on his back. They knew there was a balm in Gilead.

Notes

1. *Health Care Financing Review,* 5, No. 3, (Spring 1984) (Washington, D.C.: Office of Statistics and Data Management, Bureau of Date Management and Strategy, Health Care Financing Administration, U. S. Government Printing Office) p. 7.

2. Lewis Thomas, *The Medusa and the Snail* (New York: Bantam Books, 1979), p. 36.

3. Thomas, p. 37.

4. Fred B. Craddock, *John* (Atlanta: John Knox Press, 1982), p. 42.

5. Arthur John Gossip, *The Interpreter's Bible,* vol. 8, ed. George Arthur Buttrick (Nashville: Abingdon Press, 1952), p. 541.

6. Thomas, p. 40.

6
The Test Question:
John 6:1-14

Someone's hungry Lord, Come by here.
Someone's hungry Lord, Come by here.
Oh, Lord, Come by here.
   —"Kumbaya," African folk song

Probably no question touches our time more than
Jesus' sixth question. A multitude followed Jesus to the
other side of the Sea of Galilee. They had seen His
miracles, and they came for more. All four of the Gospels record this story. They stayed late in the day, and
they were hungry. Jesus looked out on that sea of hungry faces, and He asked, "How are we to buy bread, so
that these people may eat?" (v. 5).

What does Jesus see as He looks out at our world? The
number of Americans living below the poverty line
climbed 35 percent between 1979 and 1983. The income gap between the nation's poorest and richest citi-
zens has reached record levels.[1] The American poor
are only the tip of the iceberg. At least 750 million
people in the poorest nations live in extreme poverty
with annual per-capita incomes less than $75. Hun-
dreds of millions more in developing countries subsist
at poverty-level incomes.[2] At least 462 million are

starving, and many more do not have enough calories to do more than exist. Probably a billion persons on this globe are badly undernourished or face starvation. About forty thousand human beings die every day after an agonizing period of slow and painful starvation.[3] Does not Jesus see the hurting needs of our world?

The sixth question that Jesus raised seems, at first, to be a hunger question. The people's stomachs growled. Something had to be done. But John said that this was not a question of hunger. The Gospel of John clarifies Jesus' words to Philip: "This he said to test him" (v. 6). The issue went far beyond the problem of hunger. The response of the disciples would define who they thought He was and what their own commitment would entail.

At the end of His ministry, in the last parable He would ever give, Jesus ended His teachings with the same test. "And the King will answer them, 'Truly, I say to you, as you did it to one of the least of these my brethren, you did it to me'" (Matt. 25:40). Our Lord referred to human need: the hungry, the thirsty, the stranger, the naked, the sick, and the prisoner. Sheep and goats were separated according to how they responded to the needs at hand.

The twentieth-century church must struggle with this primary question: not how many we baptize, how large is our church, how we maintain our buildings— but, What do we do about a hurting world? The acid test is what response we make to "the least of these."

You might pause right now and ask how much you have given in the last twelve months to help a world that hurts. What percentage of your income goes to help other people? You might study your church's budget. How much of what your congregation gave last year went toward missions? What amount did your church give to help the hungry? What projects are you engaged in as a congregation to make your community a better place?

The test of any genuine faith is not what we say but what we do: "If a brother or sister is ill-clad and in lack of daily food, and one of you says to them, 'Go in peace, be warmed and filled,' without giving them the things needed for the body, what does it profit? So faith by itself, if it has no works, is dead" (Jas. 2:15-16).

Jesus first asked Philip this test question. It was understandable that Jesus turned to Philip. This disciple came from the region where they were, Bethsaida. He knew the territory. Jesus turned to the man who knew the resources of the area and asked, "How are we to buy bread, so that these people may eat?"

Philip's response was that of a pragmatist. He threw up his hands in despair. "Two hundred denarii would not buy enough bread for each of them to get a little" (v. 7). A year's wages would hardly have covered that need before him. Philip answered as many of us respond. He was a realist. This disciple saw the problem of human need as hopeless. Nothing could be done.

Philip was probably not a callous man. He probably felt much for that crowd before him. But the magnitude of the problem was too great. He was immobilized by that crowd of hungry people. The disciples' resources were not enough. He shook his head in despair.

We have all felt as Philip. We sit in our dens some evening watching television. There comes across the screen a face. It is a child: hollow eyes, shriveled, emaciated. His stomach is bloated. The announcer tells us that if all the world's truly needy lined up thirty-six inches apart outside your front door, the line would stretch out until it encircled the globe twenty-five times. The voice drones on. Fifteen to twenty million people are starving to death every year, and as many as ten million of these are children.[4] We sit there in a daze. We cannot even imagine ten million children hungry and dying. We think of our own children and our obligations—rent, groceries, the other bills we have to pay. Suddenly, we turn to another station. We do not know what to do.

Philip failed the test of human need that day on the hillside as millions of American Christians fail that same test today. Sometimes we hide behind rumors like the woman in California who was caught with sixty envelopes of food stamps. We hear about someone else on welfare driving a Cadillac. We talk to our friends about the riffraff on relief and shake our heads. But none of these excuses address the problem. Philip's response to Jesus' question was inadequate, and so are most of our answers. Despair, frustration, or pragmatism do not touch the cries of a hurting world.

Andrew must have heard the question Jesus raised. He made another reply to the question. He asked Jesus: "There is a lad here who has five barley loaves and two fish; but what are they among so many?" (v. 9).

Philip's response was to shake his head. Andrew answered with a "maybe." There would have been no miracle recorded by all four Gospels had not Andrew raised his own question. His "perhaps" literally opened up the possibility for a miracle.

The church that passes the test in our time will not be side-tracked by computer printouts and mounting figures that point to impossible needs and inadequate resources. This is not enough. Andrew went beyond pragmatism. He dared to say "perhaps": *there is a lad here.*

In 1983 more than $5,966,000 was given to hunger funds administered by one denomination. Besides this, $687,714 was given for general relief ministries.[5]

The beginnings of this response were small. Ten years ago Walker Knight, Everett Hullum, and George Sheridan produced a landmark issue of *Home Missions* magazine on world hunger. One result of that coverage was that a small church in Atlanta, Oakhurst Baptist Church, decided to take the issue seriously. A staff member of the church, Mike Weaver, helped establish a hunger committee which eventually attracted two young seminarians, Andy Loving and Gary Gunderson. By the spring of 1977, Andy and Gary had printed a small newsletter called *Seeds* and sent it out to 800 people.

In the winter of 1978, Ken Sehested joined those unpaid volunteers, and they published their first magazine. *Seeds* reflected their church's commitment to acting creatively in light of God's concern for the poor. *Seeds* single-handedly helped its denomination face the problem of world hunger. Gifts to hunger rose from less than a million dollars in 1977 to over six million in 1983. By 1984 the little magazine had received national attention from *People Magazine, Christian Science Monitor,* and *Mother Earth News.* Food banks, soup kitchens, mission projects, homeless ministries, and millions of dollars for other hunger groups have resulted from their tireless efforts. *Seeds* today has subscribers in every state and twenty-five foreign countries. Thirty skilled volunteers can be found at the Oakhurst Baptist Church every day of the week, and they have a full-time staff of seven.[6] Most of this would have never happened had not a tiny group of Andrews, in a small church in Atlanta, decided to ask their own questions.

Andrew did not have the resources at his disposal to to feed that hungry crowd. But he passed the test of human need because he refused to believe that nothing could be done.

Any church that dares to ask its own questions about a hurting world year after year through budgets, programs, and personal commitment will not fail the test that Jesus held out.

Andrew paved the way for a miracle. The lad he mentioned was brought to Jesus. The boy unfolded a tiny lunch. His mother had prepared five tiny barley loaves and two small fish. It all looked so foolish with the needs so great. Yet the world was granted a miracle that day because the little boy passed the test of human need.

The Scriptures say that Jesus broke the bread and passed it among the multitude, and all were filled. The Greek word for *filled* means that they had all they needed. And when the broken fragments were collected, twelve basketsful remained. Christ was able to take the meager resources the boy brought and make them sufficient for the destitute. William Temple has written of this story that "what is ludicrously inadequate is now ample and an abundance is left over."[7]

When the history of the church in the latter part of the twentieth century is written, we will have to answer Jesus' painful test question. What did we do in the face of the horrendous problems of our time? Did we fail the test of human compassion and world need?

Philip failed. He could not see beyond that sea of faces. Andrew raised the question, and we are all greatly in his debt. The little boy, with his loaves and fishes, gave what he had. The multitude received what they needed.

John called this story a sign. We are back to the widow. Through that pane of plain glass, we see a multitude of hungry faces given not only food for their stomachs but the Bread of life. It happened because two people long ago responded with what they had.

Notes

1. "News Digest," *Baptist Courier,* 27 Sept. 1984, p. 12.

2. Foy Valentine, "Hunger's Face and Hunger's Faces," *World Hunger Awareness/Action Guide* (Nashville: The Christian Life Commission, 1984-85), pp. 8-9.

3. Ibid., p. 9

4. *World Hunger Awareness/Action Guide,* p. 3.

5. Ibid., p. 9.

6. Gary Gunderson, *Seeds,* 10 Oct. 1984, p. 1.

7. William Temple, *Readings in St. John's Gospel* (New York: Macmillan and Company, 1955), p. 74.

7
The Offensive Question: John 6:60-71

Go on! Go on! Go on! Go on!
Go on! Go on! Go on! Go on!
Go on! Go on! Go on! Go on!
Go on! Go on! Go on! Go on!
—Hymn written by early
   American Indian convert

One of the most troublesome questions of faith is dealt with at the end of John's sixth chapter. Jesus and His disciples faced their first major crisis. After the feeding of the five thousand, that crowd came together to make Him their king. But Jesus refused their crown and fled to a quiet place on the other side of the sea to pray.

The next day the crowd came back for more bread. Jesus refused to feed them. They left as quickly as they had come. As John 6 closes, the crowds were gone. Only the disciples remained. They wonder what had gone wrong. Jesus asked His next question: "Do you also wish to go away?" (v. 67). These words deal with the dark side of discipleship—the offense that the gospel brings.

John's first readers in the first century found life hard. Many rejected Jesus outright. Some started to follow Him and turned away. Others wondered why there was

47

so much suffering and injustice and death. The early church was tempted to fall away. John told this story to help them deal with the crises in their own lives.

John told them a story of a crowd that was so much like that first century, desperately wanting Jesus' bread and His kingdom and yet so tempted to turn away. Why did those who had been fed turn away so quickly? Why had those who had tried to make Him king leave the next day? Why are disciples in every age so tempted to fall by the wayside?

John said that many turned away because Jesus would not meet their demands. They were concerned with food. They only wanted a Messiah that could give them bread everyday. They were like Jesus' mother when she asked for wine at the wedding. He did not give them what they wanted. In frustration, those five thousand abandoned Him.

John wanted his troubled readers to see that their needs went far beyond the food they craved. Jesus did not minimize the importance of daily bread. In the Model Prayer, Jesus told His followers to pray for daily bread. Jesus said the great test of faith was how disciples would respond to the physical needs around them. But at the end of that story, Jesus moved beyond physical needs. The hungry crowd could not understand.

John wrote that life was spiritual as well as physical. Jesus told them they were to feed on Him. Jesus said: "Truly, truly, I say to you, unless you eat the flesh of the Son of man and drink his blood, you have no life in you; he who eats my flesh and drinks my blood has eternal life, and I will raise him up at the last day" (v. 53). Jesus was not only concerned with their bodies but also their spirits. "It is the spirit that gives life, the flesh is of no avail; the words that I have spoken to you are spirit and life" (v. 63). Religion that answers only physical needs is like a house built on sand.

John wanted those in the first century to learn a lesson from that crowd who took offense and walked away. Every age must deal with its own response to the hard side of the gospel. Will we also go away?

Christ does far more than answer our prayers. Sometimes we pray for wine or bread. We want our everyday concerns addressed. Often we are tempted to turn away because these prayers are not answered. The bread we pray for is often not given. Like those five thousand, we wonder about His power.

Jesus speaks to the deep needs of our lives. He does not ignore our petitions or our requests. But in the Lord's Prayer when He prayed for daily bread, He had more in mind than bread for the table. Give us, He taught them, whatever it is that you need for all the things you face. Such an understanding takes our whole lives into account, not just our minimal needs. As we pray this prayer for daily bread, we begin to find an adequacy that will cover all that comes.

This seventh question forces us to remember that life has a spiritual as well as a physical side. Consequently, when we feed on Him we take into our lives a bread for all we face. There is a spiritual bread for all the hungers and thirsts of life. Let us look at two examples.

Mary comes to church on Sunday with many burdens. Her husband is slipping away. The wrinkles are coming. Her sixteen-year-old has been in trouble with the police; the girl's grades are falling. Mary's mother died last year. She is afraid and depressed. She sits in church desperately looking for help. Will it come?

Across the aisle, John folds and unfolds his bulletin nervously. Last week, he was passed over for a promotion he counted on. A younger man got the job. He is drinking almost every night. His inner life is empty. He worries about his daughter's college expenses. He wants to believe that he finds it hard to pray. He keeps coming back, Sunday after Sunday, hoping to find some answers for the dark questions of his life.

Each separate problem that John and Mary bring to church could be addressed, and both of them would still be empty. Will they turn away because Christ does not give them all they want? This is the offensive question. What Christ says to every John and Mary is that He brings a life-giving Bread that will cover all we face and enable us to deal with the hard things of our lives. This is no small miracle. Drawing on His resources, we find the Bread for all of life. Henry Drummond understood this when he wrote:

> And loving Him, you must become like Him. Love begets love. It is a process of induction. Put a piece of iron in the presence of an electrified body, and that piece of iron for a time becomes electrified. It is changed into a temporary magnet in the mere presence of a permanent magnet, and as long as you leave the two side by side, they are both magnets alike. Remain side by side with Him who loved us, and gave Himself for us, and you too will become a permanent magnet, a permanently attractive force.[1]

Our lives take on a power when we feed on the living Bread. The disciples would finally understand the offense of this question. The crowds turned away because they could not accept all He brought. He would change it all—not just the pains of their stomachs.

Through the years, the church would link their Memorial Supper celebrations with the feeding of the five thousand and the words that followed. In all the circumstances of their lives, believers have come to the table to feed on Him.

We remember, and in the remembering we are filled and changed. We leave the table, not to fall away or break under the strain but to face the troubles of our times unafraid.

Note

1. Henry Drummond, *The Greatest Thing in the World* (Mount Vernon, N.Y.: The Peter Pauper Press, n.d.) pp. 41-42.

8
The Primary Question:
John 7:25-31

There was a Man
who dwelt in the East
centuries ago
and now I cannot look
at a sheep or a sparrow,
a lily or a cornfield,
a raven or a sunset,
a vineyard or a mountain
without thinking of Him.[1]
—G. K. Chesterton

Several years ago, a religious publishing house issued copies of a painting of the face of Jesus. After the picture had been distributed at book stores and churches, the publishers began to receive complaints. Many people did not like the strong blues in the background of the picture. The colors were too bold. The painting clashed with Sunday School rooms all over the country. The editors and printers went back to work. They published a new picture with the background in neutral colors. The painting would fit any decor. The controversy subsided.

Every age has faced the task of living with the strong, bold picture of Jesus painted by the Gospel accounts, or altering the picture to suit their times and tastes. The first heresy of the church dealt with this problem. Gnosticism asked who was Jesus? Was He human or God? Was He fully human, or did He merely appear to *look* human? Could God suffer as people do?

Harold Kushner has struggled with this question in his best-seller *When Bad Things Happen to Good People*.[2] Kushner and his family learned that their three-year-old son had progeria, the disease of rapid aging. The boy would never grow taller than three feet, would have no hair on his head or body, and would die in his early teens as an old man. After the death of his son, people began to try to comfort the Kushners. They would say this had been God's will. They told the family that God took the boy to be with Him. Others said that God did this to make them better people. The grief-stricken father was horrified. He began to ask his own questions. Why would God do this to us? Is God punishing us for past sins? What could we possibly have done to merit such suffering to our child? Kushner sought to answer what kind of God was running the universe.

John sought to help his troubled age understand who Jesus was in his Gospel. His writings teach us that if we want to know what God is like we must look into the face of Jesus. There is no discontinuity.

This is the thrust of Jesus' eighth question: "You know me, and you know where I come from? But I have not come of my own accord; he who sent me is true, and him you do not know. I know him, for I come from him, and he sent me" (vv. 28-29).

We call this question primary because understanding the nature of Jesus is essential. If we answer the Jesus question, we answer the God question. In answering the question about God, we begin to answer the human question. As we learn who Jesus is, we see something of the nature of God. And in learning about God's nature, we begin to get a glimpse into who we are to be—sons and daughters of the Most High.

How did those who first heard these words answer the question about Jesus' identity? Superfically they answered His challenge in terms of heredity and environment. In John 6 they said: "Is not this Jesus, the son of Joseph, whose father and mother we know? How does he now say 'I have come down from heaven?' " (John 6:42). In John 7 His own people would say to Him: "Yet we know where this man comes from; and when the Christ appears, no one will know where he comes from" (John 7:27).

Those in Jerusalem spoke of His background. They "remembered when." They knew His brothers and sisters. They knew He came from Nazareth.

They answered the question of His identity as we sometimes answer it. Sure, we know Him. He is six feet tall. He is the carpenter's son. He did not have much formal education. He is redheaded and redbearded. He is of the house of David—strong and rugged, an outdoorsman. This Jesus had a face like theirs and a background like their own.

He could never be the Messiah. He was too familiar. "How is it that this man has learning," they muttered, "when he has never studied?" (John 7:15). He had His enemies. He came late to wedding feasts and to the holy days in Jerusalem. He looked more like their brothers and sisters than He did a god. He told stories about earthy things that did not sound religious at all. He spoke of sowing seeds and finding lost coins and sheep and boys. He sometimes became sarcastic with their leaders, the Pharisees. He would speak of unlikely things like *good* Samaritans. He disarmed them all with the peculiar manner in which He treated women with such kindness.

The crowd that heard Jesus' eighth question had a ready answer. Certainly, they knew Him—born in a stable, His mother already pregnant before the wedding. They knew. How could He possibly be the Messiah? The Messiah would do spectacular things. He would be special and different. Did not the Old Testament say that He would come out of the blue, and everybody would love Him, and the whole wide world would change?

They did not really know Him. They knew something of His heredity and environment, and in knowing that they missed the meaning of the primary question.

Who can be known simply by graphs, charts, computers, and gross national products? The elements of the human body are now worth less than ten dollars. Facts and figures alone cannot tell us who we are.

One day the insurance man will come by with a check. It will have only been a short time since the funeral. Here and there will be seen the remaining flowers, still alive in the pots. There will be a pile of sympathy cards on the coffee table. A family member may be still staying over at night. The widow will sit there fingering the check she has been given. He worked hard for forty years. They had skimped, saved, and paid for the braces and dancing lessons. They had wondered about how they would make ends meet many times. But somehow they had gotten through the teenage years, the driving lessons, dating, college education, the wedding, and even retirement. But sitting there with that check in her lap, well fixed for the first time in her whole life, she would give every dime away to have her husband back.

Heredity and environment, paychecks and neighborhoods—these things do not tell the whole story. We are all more than the sum of our parts.

The crowd that heard Jesus' eighth question had no idea who He was. They could quote Scripture and verse. They could even say the right words in describing Him. They knew their facts. But they did not know Him. They missed something very basic in the process of their knowing.

Jesus jolted them with His answer. "I have not come of my own accord; he who sent me is true, and him you do not know. I know him, for I come from him, and he sent me" (vv. 28-29).

He lived by their rules and was one of them. Yet there was more. There was this transcendent dimension. There was something more than chairs, tables, money, and laughter. Deep, deep down inside there came forth another quality: the God dimension. "I have not come on My own accord."

The crowd that day could not believe His words. They thought the Messiah was to be unknown. He would be shrouded in mystery. He would not be familiar or understood. But when Christ stood there before them, they rejected what they saw.

God, then, is like Jesus. In the heredity and environment, God works. We long for signs, miracles, fireworks, and trumpets. Instead, we are given a picture of God in Christ—utterly disarming and amazingly ordinary. George Macdonald caught a glimpse of Jesus' real nature when he wrote:

> They all were looking for a king
>   To slay their foes and lift them high;
> Thou cam'st, a little baby thing
>   That made a woman cry.[3]

If we find Him at all, we do not meet Him best in stained glass and organ music. We meet Him in the common experiences of our lives.

Let us return to that widow who sits with her grief by the window in her living room. She knows that she could never tell her own story with heredity, environment, facts, and figures. She sits there with the insurance check in her hands. She remembers her husband, who he was, not the facts. You wouldn't find what she remembers in any record book. Some thought he was gruff and difficult. He scared some of the neighbor's children. But she knew that he wasn't really like that. She remembers the first year they were married and how little they started out with. She remembers the funny way he told a story, the day he came back from the war, and how he wept that day he lost his job, out there in the backyard, when he didn't think anybody was looking. She remembers how he loved baseball, those infernal cigars, and the plowing of his garden in the springtime. The widow sees her dead husband as he really was because she saw him through a lifetime of experiences.

Jesus was not talking of doctrine when He asked, "Do you know Me?" He was talking about experience. For in the mess He was in, He made it sparkle and shine. And from Him we learn about how life can be lived on this planet in the here and the now. We, like Him, are never alone because with us and in us there is a Father who loves, sustains, cares, and forgives. We see Him through the pages of the New Testament where the cup of His life ran over with so many good things. And we begin to know that if He found some meaning and hope and joy in His days here, then we just might find those things in our living too.

He was One of us: Emmanuel, God with us (Matt. 1:23). Here is the essence of the primary question. In response, His own people asked another question. "When the Christ appears, will he do more signs than this man has done?" (John 7:31). John called them believers. The signs in their hearts could never be wrong.

Notes

1. G. K. Chesterton,

2. Harold Kushner, *When Bad Things Happen to Good People* (New York: Avon Books, 1981) pp. 1-5.

3. George Macdonald, "That Holy Thing," *Masterpieces of Religious Verse,* ed. James Dalton Morrison (New York: Harper and Brothers, 1948), p.144.

9
The Forgiveness Question: John 8:1-11

Forgiveness is the answer to the child's dream of a miracle by which what is broken is made whole again, what is soiled is again made clean. The dream explains why we need to be forgiven, and why we must forgive. In the presence of God, nothing stands between Him and us—we are forgiven. But we *cannot* feel His presence if anything is allowed to stand between ourselves and others.[1]

—Dag Hammarskjold

Half asleep at a lazy Sunday afternoon ordination council, we had gathered to screen a young man for the ministry. I was jolted awake by a question. One of the laypersons asked the preacher to be ordained: "If you were to sum up what you believe in one sentence— what would you say?" He continued: "If you were to boil it all down to the bare bones, what would be left? What is the essence of your gospel?" That question stabbed me awake. I sat there wondering that if I had been on the hot seat, how I would have answered. All the way home, I could not get that layperson's question out of my mind. What is the essence of the gospel?

John's Gospel answers the question in the eighth chapter. Many scholars say that this particular story should not even be in the text. None of the oldest manuscripts include the story. Many of the best commentaries ignore the passage altogether. Why do we deal with this story, and why did it find its way into the canon?

As the scene opens, the Lord was in the Temple teaching a crowd of people. The Scribes and Pharisees interrupted Him. They dragged in a sobbing woman, hands over her face, head down, and embarrassed. "Teacher, this woman has been caught in the act of adultery. Now in the law Moses commanded us to stone such. What do you say about her?" (v. 4). As the woman wept quietly, they glared at Jesus, waiting for His answer.

The Pharisees were sure that they had Jesus either way. If He said, "Stone her," the Romans would have charged Him for advocating murder. If He had shaken His head and said, "I will not stone her," the Jews would convict Him of heresy. What was Jesus to do?

The Fourth Gospel says that He did the strangest thing. He knelt down and wrote in the sand. And when He finally stood, Jesus said, "Let him who is without sin among you be the first to throw a stone at her" (v. 7). Once again, He bent down and wrote a second time in the sand. Beginning with the eldest, the accusers dropped their stones and crept away. Jesus and the woman were left alone. This was the setting of Jesus' ninth question: "Woman, where are they? Has no one condemned you?" (v. 10). She shook her head. Jesus said, "Neither do I condemn you; go, and do not sin again" (v. 11).

This story found its way into the heart of the church because it expresses the essence of the gospel. "Go, and do not sin again."

This forgiveness question was the centerpiece of His ministry. What do we learn about forgiveness from this beautiful story?

Forgiveness means to meet Jesus Christ firsthand. The weeping woman did not know what to expect, trembling there before His feet. Maybe He would be like all the rest: hard, mean, cruel. Maybe He would punish her as the law required.

Jesus did not say a word. Neither did He respond to the charges the officials had brought. Through her fingers she saw Him kneel and write something in the sand. We do not know what He wrote, but when He stood, He addressed the accusers: "Let him who is without sin among you be the first to throw a stone at her" (v. 7). Then He stooped down again and wrote, and as He wrote she could hear the stones dropping to the ground. When Jesus stood again, the crowd had disappeared. It was very quiet; perhaps a bird sang. She would never forget His words as long as she lived: "Woman, where are they? Has no one condemned you? . . . Neither do I condemn you; go, and do not sin again" (vv. 10-11).

Jesus did not condemn this woman. He took her seriously. He saw more than the sin, the disgrace, and the wasted years. Jesus saw a woman with a potential that she had never found.

When Jesus met her firsthand, He reached out in love and care. He took her seriously. He understood all the twisting and winding roads that had led her to that terrible hour. He knew her through and through, and He loved her. To be forgiven is, then, to meet the One who knows it all and accepts us in our sinning.

But forgiveness goes beyond this. Forgiveness means

that we are held accountable for the wrongs we have done. The woman had to face her sin. She was forced to look at her life as it was. Jesus did not brush aside the consequences of her shabby misdeeds. Immediately after this story, John 8:12 calls Jesus the "light." John said that He was the light of the world. Standing there, with the woman at His feet, the Light exposed the awful reality of who she was. There was no place to hide. She was held accountable for the wrongs of her life.

There will be no forgiveness until we face what we have done. She could not blame her sins on the man, her parents, her limited background, or the world she lived in. She was responsible. The Light always shines back into the far corners of our lives where the roaches and mice play and where the spiders spin their deadly webs. That Light hurts, and that Light heals.

When any prodigal says, "I have sinned," a miracle begins. God holds us accountable. We must face up to our responsibilities.

The Scribes and Pharisees failed to find forgiveness that day because they were unable to face their greed, their self-righteousness, and their own wrongs. The church that fails to remember they are sinners saved only by the grace of God can never know a proper forgiveness. We are all held accountable for what we have done.

This story teaches us another lesson. Forgiveness means we stand up and face the future without the weight of the past. The Pharisees wanted to stone her. They wanted to make her suffer for her misdeeds. Nothing could be done for one who had committed such a sin.

Jesus released the woman from the heavy burden of her past and showed her the door to the future. She was washed clean to begin again: "Where are they? . . . Neither do I condemn you; go, and do not sin again" (v. 11).

The burden was now on her shoulders. She could let her past fall away, or she could carry it to her dying day. John does not tell us what her response was. We assume she left that place changed and forgiven.

A woman came to see me once and told me that she was eaten up with guilt over the way she had treated someone else. She had done some terrible things to someone she loved; now that person was dead, and she could not find forgiveness. She did not know what to do. Week after week she came back, repeating the same sad story. She desperately wanted to be forgiven, but she could not feel the cleansing power of God. Finally, after many visits, I grew desperate. How could this woman understand that God would take her sins and remember them no more? So one week I took a chair, put it in front of her, and said, "God is sitting in this chair. I want you to tell Him whatever you want Him to know about how you feel about what you have done. Whatever you want to tell Him, just let it out. I'm going to sit here and listen. But I want you to talk to God and not me."

So, reluctantly, she began to pour it all out, bits and pieces of her guilt and her sin. Finally, after a long time, she seemed to be finished. I then asked her to move to the chair where God had been sitting and to sit there. Puzzled, she did this. And then I said, "Now I want God to respond to this woman and to all she has said today. What would He say if He were sitting where you sit?"

She sat there for just a minute and then said, "Can I move back into the other chair for a minute. I've got something else to tell Him." She moved, talked for just a minute, then moved back to the chair where God had been sitting. She looked for a long, long time at the chair where she had sat and confessed. Then, very lovingly, she spoke quietly. "I want to tell this woman that I know how she feels, and I know that she means it and I forgive her right now, but it will probably take her a long, long time to realize that she's forgiven." Without any coercion on my part, she moved from God's chair back into her own. Tears streamed down her face, and over and over again she said the same thing, "Wow! Wow! Wow!" This was the beginning of a splendid journey. The story is still unfolding to this day.

Jesus' ninth question is a powerful question. Enshrined in His words to another weeping woman long ago we find the essence of the gospel for us all.

Note

1. Dag Hammarskjold, *Markings* (New York: Alfred A. Knopf, 1964), p. 124.

10
The Hard Question:
John 8:21-59

When you are young, I think, your hearing is in some ways better than it is ever going to be again. You hear better than most people the voices that call to you out of your own life to give yourself to this work or that work. When you are young, before you accumulate responsibilities, you are freer than most people to choose among all the voices and to answer the one that speaks most powerfully to who you are and to what you really want to do with your life. But the danger is that there are so many voices, and they all in their ways sound so promising.[1]

—Frederick Buechner

The words of Jesus' tenth question were spoken out of frustration and despair. They were addressed to His own people, the Jews. Among that company were neighbors, friends, and religious officials.

For months the pressure had been mounting. Since John's second chapter when Jesus cast the money changers from the Temple, the lines had been clearly drawn. When He healed a paralytic on the sabbath, they muttered. He found (John 5) that He could not move comfortably in Jerusalem as He had once done. There was a contract out on His life, and once again the

crowd showed their teeth. The Pharisees met and studied the situation. The chief priests and others joined
forces to have Him arrested. The man was dangerous.
He had to be stopped. Then He fed five thousand on a
hillside, and they wanted to make Him their political
king. But it changed quickly. By the end of that sixth
chapter He looked around, and all those who had
pushed, shoved, and demanded so much had drifted
away. Only the twelve remained. By John's eighth
chapter, the Pharisees had tried once again to entrap
Him. Then the Jews plotted to kill Him. They said ugly
things to Him: "We were not born of fornication" (John
8:41). Unlike You, Jesus, we are legitimate. This was the
setting of Jesus' tenth question. "Why do you not understand what I say?" (v. 43). And their reply? "Are we not
right in saying that you are a Samaritan and have a
demon?" (v. 48). This eighth chapter finally ended with
the terrible words: "So they took up stones to throw at
him; but Jesus hid himself, and went out of the temple"
(v. 59).

What is the meaning of Jesus' hard question? "Why
do you not understand what I say?" What was it that
crowd missed, in His words and deeds, of who He truly
was?

They failed to understand that God spoke in their
time as He had spoken to Abraham long ago. The early
church, in writing later, wanted the record set straight:
"In many and various ways God spoke of old to our
fathers by the prophets; but in these last days he has
spoken to us by a Son" (Heb. 1:1-2).

Was it not strange that those believing Jews, His
friends and neighbors, did not hear that voice that was
so clear, strong, and so incredibly one with them? But

John's Gospel makes it clear that they did not hear or understand Him at all. Like people in every age, they expected God to speak differently. God's Son could not speak in human language, in a Galilean accent, or to their own time.

Years ago, in college, we would play a silly game. We would stand outside a college dorm window after dark and see a friend studying in his room. He would be at his desk with the light on. We would cup our hands and speak in a loud, booming voice: "Frank, Frank. This is the Lord. Do not pass Go. Do not collect $200. Go to Africa right now." The prank always worked. We always got a howl from the boy in the room.

But underneath the joke and the laughter, I think, standing there in the dark, we really believed that if God spoke at all He would speak in a deep, booming voice—shaking us from whatever we were doing and asking us to do something as dramatic and farfetched as leaving it all behind and heading for Africa.

The problem was: when Jesus spoke like the Galileans, in an accent they knew, for the life of them they could not believe God could be in it. If God speaks, He speaks as He has always spoken, in the middle of the mess we're in. He speaks in such an ordinary voice that we have a hard time distinguishing His voice from all the other voices. It has always been like this. Knee-deep in some assignment, project, marriage, failure, or even some decision to go to Africa, He addresses us where we are.

Remember the old story of the young man who was out in the field? It was hot, and the sun was high in the sky, and it was summer. He was behind a mule, and he was plowing. Suddenly, in the sky, fifty feet tall, there were these two great letters: *G P.* And the man—hot, tired, and bone-weary—just knew that God was speaking. He was clearly saying: "Go Preach." The yarn goes that after a couple of sermons, his new congregation wondered if their preacher hadn't misunderstood. *G P* they surmised, meant "Go Plow"—never "Go Preach" —for him.

That story has always bothered me because it implies that when God calls, He calls us not to what we already do but to some other things out there on the edge where we leave behind the sweat, the sun, the mule, and the rocks of everyday. In the Scriptures, the voice of God usually came in ordinary ways.

Tending sheep in Midian, going about his business, Moses heard God speak: "Put off your shoes from your feet, for the place on which you are standing is holy ground" (Ex. 3:5). The bush burns where we are if it burns at all.

God speaks through our lives, when He speaks. To Pharisees, chief priests, friends, and neighbors who mostly followed Him for the loaves and fishes, to all these He came.

Those who gathered around Jesus that day wanted to talk about the good old days: Abraham, the Scriptures, and what used to be. Of course, there is a place for tradition, history, and orthodoxy. But they could not hear God speak to them. They never reckoned with the fact that He speaks to us where we are in what we face. Not out of it—running away and hiding—but more like Jesus' response to His own Father's voice, setting one's face toward that difficult thing He had to do and never turning back.

From then until now, the church has been filled with

practical atheists. John 8:31 opened this account by saying: "Jesus then said to the Jews who had believed in
him." They believed in the past tense, but they found
it impossible to trust God in the present tense of their
days. They could affirm that God had spoken back
there, but they could not reckon with the truth that
God still spoke in their time to their own separate
needs. Hiding behind the tradition of Abraham and the
old Scriptures, they kept the voice of God at a safe
distance.

A young, green, sixteen-year-old boy stood under tall
Georgia pine trees one night at a campfire service. The
evening was warm. Little was said. The frogs croaked
in the distance. Fireflies buzzed. In the quiet, those
gathered watched the flickering fire. There were songs,
a story, and a prayer. But something happened. There
was no *G P* in the dark sky that night. There were no
voices. There was something more like a hunch, an
emotion, a knowing. But the call came. Words cannot
describe what happened there in the darkness by that
lake. But it was a call so deep and strong that the one
who heard it writes these lines some thirty years later.

God calls us all—not just to the ministry or to Africa,
though sometimes He does just that. So He meets us
where we are in a voice that we can grasp: I am here,
and I love you, and I will be with you always. *"Why do
you not understand what I say?"*(v. 43, Author's italics).

Life is cumbersome for most of us. Things have not
worked out as many of us have planned. Where is God?
We keep scanning the skies for some magical sign that
will take us out of the mud, sweat, heat, and pain. But
it usually does not happen that way. He is with us,
calling us to bring order out of some chaos, to find some

meaning in the grief and boredom of our everyday lives.

He comes to it all: Grief—like He came to Mary and Martha when they thought they could not go on. Sex—like that weeping woman they threw, weeping and ashamed, at His feet. Competition—like those two power-hungry brothers, James and John, so greedy. Sickness—like that broken man who sat with vacant eyes by the pool of life year after year. Jesus spoke to them all, but never in the same voice. He spoke to their needs and to whatever would bring healing to their broken lives.

The world is full of people like those Jews and Pharisees who missed who He was. We find it hard to hear the great voices that come. We have listened to the tiny voices so long that our lives are shallow and empty. We run the terrible risk of spending all our days on the inconsequential, skimming around the edges of life. And one day some family will stand by some open grave the way Biff does at the grave of his dad in *Death of a Salesman.* But Biff can't cry. It hurts too much. The only thing the boy can say, over and over again is, "He didn't know who he was. He didn't know who he was."[2]

But some of us do understand what He says. Have you ever been dragged along to a concert, knowing little or nothing about music? The lights dim, the curtain rises, the maestro comes out, and it all begins. All the instruments play music written two or three hundred years before. But you can't hear it. Your back gets stiff from the seats, and you shift in your place. You try to see what time it is in the darkness. Next to you, on the edge of her seat, head forward—with a wisp of a smile on her face, she hears something you've never heard. She knows the music and what the instruments are to do. Her spirit soars while you sit there missing most of what is being played. You can't hear or understand the music at all.

But she hears. That hearing did not come easily. It took her years of piano study—the theory and practice, practice, practice—for her to sit there on the edge of her seat listening to what is really there.

The principle is the same for those of us who long to hear the voice of God. It will take work and years for us to hear that great voice calling us to service. It will not happen easily. We open a Bible and read. We pray, not only in desperation but day after day. We find our way to some church to worship and to learn. We give an offering. We volunteer to teach a class of squirming kids. We ask God, again and again, to take what we are and make it count. Who knows when it happens? Along the way we find ourselves beckoned, spoken to, addressed.

This is the great promise of the gospel. Jesus' tenth question need not be our question. In our mud, sweat, and rocks we hear, and we respond.

Notes

1. Frederick Buechner, *The Hungering Dark* (New York: The Seabury Press, 1969), pp. 28-29.

2. Arthur Miller, *The Death of a Salesman* (New York: The Viking Press, 1949), p. 138.

11
The Discipleship Question:
John 9:1-11

Once I was blind, but now I can see:
The Light of the world is Jesus.
                    —Philip P. Bliss

John's ninth chapter continues the theme which began in chapter 8. There Jesus said: "I am the light of the world; he who follows me will not walk in darkness, but will have the light of life" (v. 12). Chapter 9 opens with a blind man sitting by the roadside with his tin cup begging. He had been blind all his life. Jesus came by, took spittle and clay, mixed them, and touched the man's sightless eyes. Jesus then told the man to go and wash in the pool of Siloam. The man born blind came back seeing. The Light of the world had done His work.

His neighbors could not believe it: "Is not this the man who used to sit and beg?" (v. 8). They couldn't be sure. They argued among themselves. Everybody knew that the blind did not recover their sight, and beggars remained beggars forever. But this man, standing before them, insisted: "The man called Jesus made clay and anointed my eyes and said to me, 'Go to Siloam and wash; so I went and washed and received my sight" (v. 11).

The crowd had to be sure. So they dragged him off to see the Pharisees. Surely these important officials could settle this matter. They made it sound like some kind of a crime: this man said he was blind and now he can see. The Pharisees wrinkled their brows, pursed their lips, whispered among themselves. They asked the man to repeat his story. They tried to act interested as he told all the details. The only thing they heard was that Jesus had healed him on the Sabbath day. They asked him again, and the man repeated the words: last sabbath day. Again they huddled in conference and shook their heads. They had to get to the bottom of this troublesome matter.

So they called the man's parents. You can almost see the mother wiping her hands on her apron, patting her hair in place, looking in the mirror a last time. The father left his animals and wondered what in the world the Pharisees would ask. They were simple people. They were not used to talking to Pharisees. The poor parents were scared to death. "Is this your son, who you say was born blind? How then does he now see?" (v. 19). Twisting their hands, they finally said: "Ask him; he is of age, he will speak for himself" (v. 21).

With a sigh, the Pharisees met a second time with the man who claimed to be healed. Slowly, they went through the whole unlikely sounding story again. Maybe they had missed something the first time around. Maybe the man had left out some detail they could hang him with. They asked everything. Wasn't Jesus a hoax, some kind of a fraud? Could it be that He was a sinner? The man held his ground. The longer he talked the worse it got: "If this man was not from God, he could do nothing" (v. 33). It was more than they

could take. They cast him out. The man seemed to have
lost everything as a result of his healing. His vocation as
a beggar was over. His neighbors were confused. His
parents were intimidated. His leaders were enraged by
his words. He had lost it all—his work, his home, and his
synagogue.[1] John's Gospel says that "Jesus heard that
they had cast him out, and . . . found him" (v. 35).

Three important truths shine from this story. First,
light comes to darkness. In those first verses Christ
came to the man in his blindness. Thirty-five verses
later, Christ, the Light, came again to the same man.

Light always comes to darkness. We never find Him
—He finds us. Genesis 1:1 begins: "In the beginning
God." God created the world. God took the initiative in
making male and female. And when they broke His
rules in the garden, God was there. Light always comes
to darkness.

He finds us. The old joke goes: "Have you found
God?" And someone answers: "I didn't know He was
lost." The joke is right. John says that the Lord Jesus
took the initiative. "Jesus heard that they had cast him
out, and . . . found him" (v. 35). William Temple has said
that these words expressed the greatest truth of the
Christian faith: Christ finds us.[2]

Light comes to darkness. We can't see. We don't
know where to go. We are trapped in our spiritual
blindness. And God reveals Himself. The Light comes
to our darkness. He does for us what we can never do
for ourselves.

Helen Keller knew this truth. Blind, deaf, mute—she
had been cut off from so much of the world at eighteen
months by a terrible fever. Her parents could do little
to help her. Her condition seemed hopeless. All the

neighbors thought the little Keller girl was either mad or retarded. It took someone half-blind herself, barely twenty-one, to be the wounded healer. She came to Tuscumbia, Alabama, to teach Helen. Everybody said Annie Sullivan was crazy to even try. But she came and kept at it until one shining day little deaf, mute, blind Helen began to make the connections. Years later, Helen Keller, then a world citizen of great distinction, would write:

> To this day I cannot command the uses of my soul or stir my mind to action without the memory of the quasi-electric touch of Teacher's fingers upon my palm.[3]

Annie Sullivan opened a door for Helen that would never be shut again. Helen would never say, "I found it." She would say that light came to darkness—that she was found. *He* isn't lost. *We* are. He comes to us as He came to that blind man years ago. John 1:5 says: "The light shines in the darkness."

But there is another principle embedded in Jesus' eleventh question. After the healing and all the harassment the man had felt, Christ came to him a second time. He asked the man a question: "Do you believe in the Son of man?" (v. 35). Jesus' question here is a discipleship question. The Light has come: Will you accept it? Jesus really asked the man: Will it be Light or darkness for you? "Do you believe in the Son of man?"

John loved to use this word *believe* when he spoke of Jesus. Again and again, John used a very personal definition when he spoke of belief. These words were not some intellectual exercise. Jesus really asked: Do you trust Me? Do you love Me? Will you follow Me? These are discipleship questions.

Discipleship always goes beyond the head—it also takes in the heart. Light cannot scatter the darkness of our lives if it does not begin to penetrate all we are. "You shall love the Lord your God with all your heart, and with all your soul, and with all your mind" (Matt. 22:37). Our whole beings are bound up in moving toward the Light.

We can refuse the Light just as Helen could have refused the help of her teacher. She could have remained stubborn or afraid. But Helen made a far better choice. She gave herself up to the light that came, and it altered her life immeasurably. The blind man in the story had to decide if he would give himself to Light or darkness. We have the same decision. To stand before the crossroads of Light and darkness is one of the large strands in the discipleship question.

John records that the once-blind man teaches us another lesson about discipleship: darkness can turn to Light. He fell down and worshiped Jesus. That decision was not easy for this man. The Light came gradually. Early in John 9, the disciples called Jesus "Rabbi." (v. 2). The healed man said Jesus was a man (v. 11). Later he called Jesus a prophet (v. 17). Toward the end of the chapter you can almost hear the sound of a trumpet: " 'Lord, I believe'; and he worshiped him" (v. 38). Darkness turned to Light slowly but surely. That is the definition of real discipleship.

This image of darkness to light became a symbol of conversion for the early church. As early as the second century, in the catacombs the Christians left their doctrines scratched on the walls of those hollowed-out tunnels. One of their earliest frescos for baptism was the healing of a blind man.

Here is the heart of discipleship, to have one's eyes opened. To believe with all we are in this Son of man, Jesus. To let the Light so fill up the house of life until all the rooms know healing and the places of the heart are touched with His brightness.

Notes

1. William Hull, *The Broadman Bible Commentary*, vol. 9 (Nashville: Broadman Press, 1970), p. 301.

2. William Temple, *Readings in Saint John's Gospel* (New York: Macmillan and Co. Ltd., 1955), p. 160.

3. Joseph P. Lash, *Helen and Teacher* (London: Allen Lane, 1980), p. 3.

12
The Life Question:
John 11:1-27

I would like to believe when I die that I have given myself away like a tree that sows seeds every spring and never counts the loss, because it is not loss, it is adding to future life. It is the tree's way of being. Strongly rooted perhaps, but spilling out its treasure on the wind.[1]

—May Sarton

Jesus' twelfth question is a life question. He uttered these words in a cemetery. Lazarus had died. Days before, Jesus had received word that His good friend was very sick. By the time Jesus appeared at Bethany, he had been dead four days. One of Lazarus' sisters, Martha, met Jesus when He arrived: "Lord, if you had been here, my brother would not have died" (v. 21).

Jesus addressed the heartbroken Martha. "Your brother will rise again" (v. 23). Martha knew that. She believed in the resurrection. She was a good Jew. "I know," she said, "that he will rise again in the resurrection at the last day" (v. 24). In the place of death, Jesus uttered a powerful statement: "I am the resurrection and the life; he who believes in me, though he die, yet shall he live, and whoever lives and believes in me shall never die. Do you believe this?" (v. 26).

78

Do we believe that Jesus brings life not only in the hereafter, but to the present? Do we believe that He is lifebringer and that whenever He touches, death vanishes and life flourishes?

So much in our time, like that scene in Bethany, has the stench of death about it. Yeats speaks for our age: "Things fall apart, the center cannot hold."[2] Death is everywhere. Marriages strain, crack, split, and shatter into a hundred terrible pieces. Millions in Africa face death by starvation. Drug addiction continues to soar. We continue to stockpile nuclear weapons in the name of life. *Burnout* is an eighties word that describes the numbness, the ennui that millions face everyday. We live in a world surrounded by death. The dead Lazarus is a symbol of our time.

Jesus came to that scene of death. The sisters, Mary and Martha, wept openly. Their neighbors and friends grieved. Jesus could not constrain Himself. John wrote that Jesus, too, wept. He was touched by the death of his good friend, the grief of the sisters, and the kind of a world where death was so pervasive and powerful.

But Jesus moved beyond His tears and grief. He spoke to the two sisters and then made His way to the tomb. There He called Lazarus back from the dead.

This is the seventh and last sign in the Fourth Gospel. What are we to learn as we peer through this window of understanding? Jesus brings life. Where Jesus is, there is resurrection, and resurrection always means life. Martha recognized this with her words: "Lord, if you had been here, my brother would not have died" (v. 21). But she revealed much more when she answered Jesus' twelfth question: Martha, do you believe that I am the resurrection and the life?

William Temple has said that Martha, in her response, made the fullest confession found in this Gospel up to this point.[3] She called Him Lord, Christ, Son of God, the One who was coming into the world. Martha, through her tears, discovered firsthand that whenever Jesus came, He brought life. Resurrection, then, was not only some doctrine for some future time. Christ brought abundant life for the present as well.

Lazarus is a symbol of so much of the world as it is—dead and decaying. Martha is a symbol of what could happen to us all if we answer this twelfth question. "Do you believe this?" (v. 26).

Have we learned this larger definition of resurrection? Jesus brings new life to the present and the future. Do *we* believe this?

Do we see Him as life giver in our everyday lives? The church has been reading these words about life for centuries, and little seems to change.

Carson McCullers indicts the modern church in her novel *Clock Without Hands.* In that book, J. T. Malone, a druggist in a small southern town, discovers that he is dying of leukemia. In desperation he turns to Dr. Watson, his pastor at the First Baptist Church, for some answers. The conversation never gets off the ground. Dr. Watson is threatened by the gloomy talk of his parishioner. He hides behind the words of his faith to keep distance between himself and the dying Malone. The druggist finally leaves the pastor's house empty and alone.[4]

Eternal life begins now. A. T. Robertson said that John 11:26 should be translated: He that believeth in

Me "shall not die forever."[5] This was a strong double negative of reassurance. So much of our preaching and living ignores Jesus' promise for the present. Those who discover the new life that Martha found can face the present with confidence and creativity.

When the great organist E. Power Biggs died, he had graced many churches with his great gift as a musician. At his memorial service, his cousin read some words that summarized a life of meaning and purpose:

> Everyone must leave something behind when he dies. A child or a book or a painting or a house or a wall built or a pair of shoes made. Or a garden planted. Something your hand touched some way so your soul has somewhere to go when you die, and when people look at that tree or that flower you planted, you're there. It doesn't matter what you do, so long as you change something from the way it was before you touched it into something that's like you after you take your hands away. The difference between the man who just cuts lawns and a real gardener is in the touching. The lawncutter might just as well not have been there at all; the gardener will be there a lifetime.[6]

The resurrection that Jesus talked of meant life for the present and the future.

So the future tense of our belief in the resurrection cannot be ignored. Just as we face the present unafraid and confident, we can also face death with the certainty of faith.

Dr. Herbert Gezork was the longtime president of the Andover-Newton Theological Seminary. After his retirement he moved to Vero Beach, Florida, to live out his last years. Dr. Gezork became very ill and was taken to the hospital for the last time. After days of excruciating illness, his pastor was with him at the end. As life slipped away, Dr. Gezork's last words were, "It is more beautiful than anything I ever dreamed." Resurrection is a word for death as well as life.

Peer through the window of this twelfth question. Look long and hard at Jesus—His resurrection and His life. Those that look long enough will discover what Martha came to know. He is the resurrection and the life for today and for all the days that come. And when the days are over and the journey finally ends, He will be there, too.

Notes

1. May Satron, *Recovering* (New York: Norton, 1980), p. 140.

2. William Butler Yeats, "The Second Coming," quoted in *Bartlett's Familiar Quotations*, 125th ed., ed. Emily Morison Beck (Boston: Little, Brown and Co., 1980), p. 714.

3. William Temple, *Readings in Saint John's Gospel* (London: Macmillan, 1955), p. 182.

4. Carson McCullers, *Clock without Hands* (New York: Bantam Books, 1963), pp. 138-140.

5. A. T. Robertson, *Word Pictures in the New Testament,* vol. 5 (Nashville: Sunday School Board of the SBC, 1932), p. 200.

6. Ray Bradbury, *Fahrenheit 451,* (New York: Simon and Schuster, 1967), n.p.n.

13
The Human Question: John 12:20-36

Here there met the horror of death and the ardour of obedience.[1]

—Bengel

Life is a series of doors that open and close. Sometimes the doors slam with a bang. Other times doors close so quietly that we do not know when the event occurs. We close and open doors all our lives.

Exits are often painful. Saying good-bye to the past, people, and places we love always brings grief. Little children cry for last year's teacher. The old long for a familiar voice and the touch of a vanished hand. Like Israel, we wistfully look back to some Egypt—settled, familiar, and safe. Ernest Hemingway wrote, "We all have a favorite girl, and her name is nostalgia." Most of us find exits difficult.

But entrances, too, are filled with tension. The new can be frightening and foreboding. The yet-to-be is uncertain, painful and difficult. To open a door to a new work, a new chapter, or a new adventure usually always brings anxiety. The people of God imagine the giants of the not-yet are ten feet tall. We prefer the comfort of yesterday. Entrances make us nervous.

Jesus' thirteenth question is a very human question.
A door was closing, and another door—unknown and
dark—was beginning to open. After this question, all
would be different. His destiny would be sealed. His
public ministry would be behind Him forever.

After Jesus had raised Lazarus from the dead, he
moved to the eye of the storm. He entered Jerusalem
as a glorious King amid shouts and hallelujahs and palm
branches. That Palm Sunday was such a success that the
Pharisees shook their heads and muttered, "The world
has gone after him" (v. 12).

A company of Greeks came to meet Him. Either they
had been in that Palm Sunday crowd, or they had heard
of Jesus' work and power. They came to see for themselves. They spoke to Philip, but this Greek disciple did
not know what to do. He turned to Andrew, and together they approached Jesus about the Greek delegation.

The door began to close. Would Jesus go to the
Greeks now that His own leaders plotted His death?
Would He shake the dust off His feet and enter a new
door symbolized by the Greek's interest? To leave His
own people and the conflict may have been as tempting
as those temptations in the wilderness years before.

What was right and what was wrong? Who could be
sure? He must have wondered about the elusive will of
God. Jesus thirteenth question was a human question.
He prayed: "Now is my soul troubled. And what shall
I say? 'Father, save me from this hour'?" (John 12:27).

To minister to the Greeks would have spared His life.
Was this God's way of saving Him from the cross He saw
so clearly on the horizon? Should He not walk through
this new door of opportunity and ministry?

"What shall I say?" was a very human question. Here

we see the humanity of the Word "made flesh" (John 1:14, KJV) fully expressed. He stood before the doors of His life, and had to decide what to do.

Jesus is one with us as we stand before our own doors of wonder and fear. He said, "Now is my soul troubled." That word *trouble* appears several times in this Gospel. It was used when Jesus saw Mary weeping for her dead brother, Lazarus (11:33). In John 13, in the upper room, Jesus used this word a third time as Judas slipped out to betray Him (13:21). The human question is a troublesome question. It always produces tension and anxiety.

Our doors are many and varied. What major is best for me? What job should I take? Whom should I marry? Shall we have a baby now? Should I leave this place for another place? What is right, and what is wrong? What if he dies? When my heart flutters and my arms tingle and I am afraid, what in the world will I do? *What shall I say?* This is a very human question.

William Barclay said that Jesus moved from tension to triumph in this passage.[2] Jesus would allow the door to His past to close, but He would not walk through the doors the Greeks had opened. There was another door: "And what shall I say? 'Father, save me from this hour'? No, for this purpose I have come to this hour. Father, glorify thy name" (v. 27).

The opening of this new door was difficult. This would be the hardest thing Jesus would ever do. To open that door meant trial, suffering, and the certainty of death. But Jesus opened this new door and walked through that portal with confidence.

What was Jesus' secret that kept Him going through this very trying period? Jesus found His answer on His knees. Every major decision of our Lord was made in prayer. After His baptism, He prayed as His ministry began. When the crowds gathered for healing and love, He slipped away into the hills to pray. When the dark shadows of the cross fell across His life, Jesus spoke to His Heavenly Father. He prayed out of His humanity. He brought to that place of prayer all He felt—the questions and troubles of His life.

We, too, are to bring our fears, disappointments, and questions to the place of prayer. And we will find the strength to close and open doors with the help of a loving Father.

In the early 1800s, Philip Doddridge lost his little son in death, and he wrote these lines in his diary:

> This day my heart hath been almost torn in pieces by sorrow; yet sorrow so softened and sweetened, that I number it among the best days of my life! . . . Doest thou well to be angry for the gourd? God knows I am not angry; but sorrowful He surely allows me to be . . . Lord, give unto me a holy acquiescence of soul in Thee; and, now that my gourd is withered, shelter me under the shadow of Thy wings.[3]

Jesus found His answer because that troubled day when the Greeks came was not an isolated experience. All His life, Jesus had been tempted. All His life, He had stood before the closing and the opening of some door. And all His life, He had sought the will of the Father. The hour of death found Him prepared because He had lived for no other purpose than the offering of Himself up to God. We need Jesus' commitment of purpose.

Doors closed and doors opened, but Jesus was never alone. "Then a voice came from heaven, 'I have glorified it, and I will glorify it again' " (v. 28). God spoke. But that voice was not easy to understand. John wrote that some throught it thundered. Others were sure they had heard an angel. Jesus knew differently. He faced a new door, hard and cumbersome, but He walked through it unafraid. He was not alone. God was there.

Doors still close and open for us all. They are always troublesome and difficult. Those that live with the human question will discover what the author of the Hebrews learned, years later, as he looked into the face of Jesus:

> For we have not a high priest who is unable to sympathize with our weaknesses, but one who in every respect has been tempted as we are, yet without sin. Let us then with confidence draw near to the throne of grace, that we may receive mercy and find grace to help in time of need (4:15-16).

Notes

1. William Barclay, *The Gospel of John,* vol. 2 (Philadelphia: The Westminster Press, 1956), p. 146.

2. William Barclay, *Gospel of John,* pp. 146-147.

3. Arthur Gossip, *The Interpreter's Bible,* vol. 8, ed. George A. Buttrick (Nashville: Abingdon, 1952), p. 665.

14
The Servant Question:
John 12:12-20

If you love Him, why not serve Him?
If you love Him, why not serve Him?
Soldiers of the cross.

—Folk Song

When I was growing up in Columbus, Georgia, we rode buses a lot. We lived four miles from downtown, so we would hop a bus on Thirty-eighth Street, ride down to Twelfth Street and Broadway and get off. But about Twentieth Street sometimes, the bus would stop in an old neighborhood with crumbling houses, and an old black woman would hobble up the steps. She was always dressed in the same way—white gloves, white shoes, and stockings. She wore a long, white satin robe that hung down to her white patent leather slippers. Many times I would see this old woman and wonder about her. One day I asked Nancy, our maid, "Who is this woman, and why does she dress so strangely?" Nancy said, "She sanctified." I didn't know what she meant, and I wasn't about to let her know I didn't know what sanctified meant. What I did was to connect that old woman with the satin robe with the word *sanctification.* To be sanctified, I reasoned, meant to be special, different, and more than a little strange. I wasn't comfortable with this word.

Jesus' fourteenth question deals with the sanctification problem. We find this question at the beginning of John 13. John used chapters 13 through 17 to prepare the church for the first major crisis they would face: what would happen when Jesus left the earth.[1] So these five chapters get us ready for the end: Good Friday, Easter morning, and the ascension.

As the thirteenth chapter opens, Jesus gathered with his disciples in the upper room to celebrate their last supper together. In the middle of the meal, Jesus took a basin and a towel and washed their feet. This was a common custom in a dusty land. Every house had a slave to remove the sandles and wash the grime from the guests' feet. Jesus' action disarmed them all. He did what the disciples did not do—servant's work. One by one, our Lord washed their feet that night.

When the Lord had finished, He poured out that very dirty water, wiped His hands clean, and returned to the head table. Then came His fourteenth question: "Do you know what I have done to you?" (v. 12).

He had washed each disciple's feet. He had patiently cleansed them one by one. Here we run headlong into that doctrine that the church today talks little about: *sanctification.* This is a John Wesley word, a Methodist word, a Pentecostal word. Sanctification means to be set apart, cleansed, washed pure. Disciples' feet get dirty. They have to be cleansed. We have largely ignored this idea of apron, basin, and towel. We feel little need for sanctification. We were baptized one time, and that should be enough for anybody. Sanctification

smacks of some old woman in a long white robe going
a bit too far in her faith.

Jesus, in washing His followers' feet, was dealing with
the essentials of discipleship. His action was so simple
we miss the profundity of His deed. To be sanctified
means to allow Him to wash the dirt away.

Simon Peter is one with us. He had been baptized.
He had already had his share of the water. "Lord," he
said, "do you wash my feet?" (v. 6). But Simon was
stubborn. "You shall never wash my feet" (v. 8). Jesus
acted as if He did not hear a word that Peter said. He
took off Peter's old, beat-up sandals and placed the big,
long, ugly feet in the basin and slowly washed off the
dirt of the day. Jesus quietly said, "What I am doing you
do not know now, but afterward you will understand"
(v. 7).

After what? After Peter had drawn a sword to protect his Lord. *After what?* After Peter had cursed three
times before a campfire and denied his Lord. *After
what?* After Peter had hidden in a locked room with
the others to save his own skin. *After what?* After Easter when he went fishing. *After what?* After a vision on
a rooftop when Peter had refused to follow God's com-
mand. Simon Peter would remember the terrible
words: "You are not all clean" (see vv. 10-11).

Some scholars believe that following that evening in
the upper room, the early church gathered each year
on the Thursday before Easter to remember. They
called that event the reconciliation of the penitents. All
those that had broken their vows and failed to live up
to their Christian commitments came back every year
with bowed heads and tears in their eyes to find cleansing again.

Here is sanctification at its best. We all get dirty. The grime of everyday collects. Christ must continually wash us clean. He takes all the sins we commit after baptism and washes the dirt of our lives away.

This word *sanctification* means to make us one with the human family. After our failures and after our sins, He comes with His basin and towel. Jesus does this terribly disarming thing: He washes away all the wrongs that smudge and disorder our lives. And, like Peter, we are prepared for the work that we have been called to do. He has left us an example: "You also ought to wash one another's feet" (v. 14). He washed us clean so that we can turn our attention to a larger world. We need to help one another stay clean.

Is there a more-needed word? Every age longs to be served. No one wants to do the serving. We are barraged today with teachers' rights, employees' rights, women's rights, and children's rights. Equality is at the heart of the gospel: "There is neither slave nor free, there is neither male nor female; for you are all one in Christ Jesus" (Gal. 3:28-29). The Scriptures were never given to keep people in chains or to starve employees from decent wages. At the same time, the best teachers we have known served their pupils. The best deacons in any church do not stalk around asking for privileges. We remember an upper room when our Lord took a basin and a towel and left us our marching orders. We wash the dirt from someone else because Someone has washed away the dirt from our lives. Here is the essence of discipleship: to be a servant to another in the loving name of Jesus.

Carlyle Marney told a beautiful story about his friend Blake Smith who was pastor at the First Baptist Church,

Austin, Texas. Smith was dying in the hospital. He asked his neighbor, the Roman Catholic priest, to come and talk with him about his fears and the failures of his life. The priest came and listened. When Smith had finished, the priest prayed for him and asked God to forgive him and take away all the dirt and sin before he slipped into the mystery. When the priest finished, he knelt down by the Baptist preacher's bed and said, "Now I want you to hear my confession." And the dying Baptist preacher nodded and listened as the priest told, in halting words, of his own failures and sins. Old, dying Blake Smith, in a broken voice, prayed and asked God to forgive the priest of all the wrongs he had committed.

Do you know what I have done to you? I have washed you clean as a newborn baby once again, that you might leave renewed, sanctified, ready to go out and wash somebody else's dirt away. Sanctification is not a strange word after all. It is basic to our understanding of commitment.

Note

1. Fred B. Craddock, *John* (Atlanta: John Knox Press, 1982), p. 97.

15
The Personal Question: John 14:1-14

I don't know how a Polaroid camera works. You put in the film, snap the picture, and wait. After counting to ten you pull out some film. At first, you think nothing has happened. The film is grey, and there is no picture. But as the light exposes the film, slowly an image appears. At first the picture is hazy and indistinct. As the seconds tick by, the picture you took becomes clearer. You keep looking, and finally you see what was there in the first place. Something like that happened to Thomas and the others. Slowly, over a period of time, they learned who Jesus was. They began to see clearly for themselves. It did not happen all at once. As they exposed themselves to the Light, slowly the truest image there ever was began to form.

—Roger Lovette

Do you remember how God looked to you when you were a little child? When I was nine years old, I could describe God's features in great detail. God was big, and His size made Him scary. He kept books on everything I did. If I was mean, He would punish me; if I did good things, He would like me. He was Father Time, my grade school principal, a little like my own father. Other days I saw Him as a combination Santa Claus, the foreman at the mill, and the policeman on the corner. God was white, a Baptist, spoke with a southern accent, and was one-hundred-percent American. He was on our side, our copilot and the Man upstairs. He seemed a million miles away.

In my college years, all this was shattered by J. B. Phillips's *Your God Is Too Small.* That book hit me like a thunderbolt. My collage of God suddenly fell apart.

The disciples found their own pictures of God transformed as they walked with Jesus. One day they finally understood the implications of His ministry. Jesus called them aside. They had been with Him when He had called Lazarus back from the grave and seen the ugly reaction of the crowd. They had heard the growing rumors of Jesus' death. He had tried to prepare them in that upper room when He broke the bread, washed their feet, and warned of betrayal. Still they were worried.

He called them together and spoke to their concerns: "Let not your hearts be troubled; believe in God, believe also in me" (14:1). He was going away, He said. They were not to be afraid. Thomas did not quite understand, but it was Philip that forced from Jesus His next question. "Lord," Philip said, "show us the Father, and we shall be satisfied" (v. 8).

Jesus must have been frustrated. We can hear the edge in his voice: "Have I been with you so long, and yet you do not know me, Philip?" (v. 9). Jesus then gave this disciple what Arthur Gossip has called the most staggering saying to be found in human literature:[1] "He who has seen me has seen the Father" (v. 9). When we see Jesus, we encounter the very face of God.

Philip demanded some proof of God. He wanted

some sign to hold on to when the night was dark, when he was afraid, when Jesus had gone.

Our age also places great value on evidence. If you visit New York's Lincoln Center you will find two huge murals in the lobby of the new Metropolitan Opera House. Each covers a space thirty-by-thirty-six feet. One wonders how the artist could have painted such magnificent panels. In the corner, with a flourish, the artist signed his name: Marc Chagall.

Philip's complaint was that God left no autograph. He seemed so hazy and indistinct. Philip begged for some miracle, some proof that could settle the faith business once and for all. Jesus told Philip that faith does not come in dazzling miracles but in human flesh.[2]

God did not sign His paintings with a flourish. He left us, instead, a Person: the Word made flesh. Jesus' life and ministry shows us clearly the character of God.

Jesus' question was: Do you not know Me, Philip? We encounter this word *know* once again. Jesus used this word many times in this Gospel. This *knowing* was a personal word.

His followers looked to the heavens for some sign of God. Finding no answer, they looked all around them for some signature of His presence. The incarnation forced them to change their direction. "He who has seen me has seen the Father" (v. 9).

God, then, is like Jesus Christ. As they looked at Him, they saw the face of God. It would take years for them to fathom the depths of those words. But, looking back, a new picture of God began to form.

Much later, Philip surely remembered that shining day when he had left all to follow Jesus. He looked back on the kindness and the acceptance that Jesus had brought into his life. Surely, he reasoned, God must be something like his Lord.

The picture must have grown larger as he remembered that other day when the Lord fed five thousand. There wasn't enough food to go around, and when they had turned to Philip, Philip had had no answers. But Jesus had taken the bits and pieces of a little boy's lunch and worked a miracle. Philip wondered if God could not take the bits and pieces of all we bring and use them many times over?

The picture became clearer. He remembered the upper room and Jesus stooping to wash his dirty feet. Was not God the Suffering Servant to His own people?

But there were larger memories. There was the cross with its terrible pain and Easter with all its hopeful wonder. Did not God suffer as did His son, and did He not come back after the worst, invading the world with His power and His love?

Philip must have remembered. Legend has it that this disciple ministered in places as scattered as Lydia, Parthia, and Gaul. Almost all agree that Philip became one of the great lights for the faith in Asia.[3]

Years before, Jesus said: "Come and see" (1:39). Philip had done just that. He found more than he ever expected. Like that character in *Winterset*, Philip could have replied: "I came here seeking light in darkness . . . and stumbled on a morning."[4]

John included this story in his Gospel years later, when he wrote to a struggling church. Rome had persecuted and killed many of the faithful. Most of the eyewitnesses had died out. The church needed some evidence of the presence of God in a hard and trying world.

John turned them toward the story of Philip and Jesus. It was the account of a man who, through the years, had learned to put his old pictures aside for something better. He had found his morning, for him it was enough.

Notes

1. Arthur Gossip, *The Interpreter's Bible*, vol. 8, ed. George A. Buttrick (Nashville: Abingdon, 1952), p. 704.

2. William E. Hull, *The Broadman Bible Commentary*, vol. 9, ed. Clifton J. Allen (Nashville: Broadman, 1970), p. 335.

3. William Barclay, *The Master's Men* (Nashville: Abingdon, 1980), p. 91.

4. Maxwell Anderson, "Winterset," *Four Verse Plays* (New York: Harcourt, Brace & World, Inc., 1959), p. 127.

16
The Continuing Question:
John 16:29-33

Faith is standing in the darkness, and a hand is there,
and we take it.[1]

—Frederick Buechner

One of the first questions in the Book of John is a faith
question. Jesus asked Nathanael if he believed. This is
understandable. The Christian journey begins with
trust and belief. Real conversion must ever struggle
with the matter of faith.

What is more puzzling is that the faith question sur-
faces again in John's sixteenth chapter. Jesus' audience
here was His own disciples. "Do you now believe?"
(16:31).

They must have bristled at this question. But Jesus
knew them well. He was familiar with their petulance,
their egocentricity, and their weaknesses. He may have
wondered if they would be able to survive the hard
times that would come. He explained the reason for His
hard words: "I have said all this to you to keep you from
falling away" (16:1).

Always, in the circle, there was a Judas who would
betray. There were a Simon, James, and John who
would sleep through it all. There was a Thomas who, for

the life of him, doubted most days. One Gospel records, "They all forsook him and fled" (Mark 14:50). Even after Easter, John Mark would abandon the first missionary journey. Demas, with Paul in prison, would forsake his companion and return to Thessalonica.

Denial and doubt is an ever-present problem for the believer. Take any church roll and run your fingers down that long, long list of inactive members. The problem of drifting, of losing one's first love, is a very real part of the pilgrim journey.

We must answer the faith question many times. At every juncture of the road we are to ponder Paul's sad warning, "Therefore let any one who thinks that he stands take heed lest he fall" (1 Cor. 10:12). Only a strong faith can sustain the twists and turns of the rocky road.

Jesus dealt with the problem of denial and doubt continually. He spoke of houses built on sand or rock. He talked of ears that hear and those that did not. His warnings tumbled out: sheep or goats, talents buried in the sand, virgins with little oil in their lamps. Through it all He asked: Will your resources be able to sustain you to the end? *"Do you now believe?"*(v. 31, Author's italics).

Very soon the greatest test of their commitment would loom before them. There would be a garden, flickering torches, and finally Calvary. Could they handle the dark side of life? Would their faith be adquate? Here we deal with a continuing question.

There is an inadequate faith that will not survive because it knows everything. Such a faith does not listen. It has all the answers. This world system is closed. The universe is inflexible. Inadequate faith demands that the church give easy answers to the troubled questions.

A faith with too many answers is like a house with the windows nailed shut, the drapes drawn, the doors locked tightly from the inside. No light shines in. The place is a fortress. Defensiveness is its stance. One can live in such a place, but it has little room for wholeness or growth.

Inadequate faith is flawed because it is overconfident. Simon Peter is a good symbol of such a faith. During the Last Supper, he boasted to Jesus: "I will lay down my life for you" (John 13:37). Simon would have been a good American. Most of us think we can handle all our problems. We need no one. We rely on ourselves and our own abilities. The little engine in the children's story has become the role model for many: We can because we *think* we can! Overconfidence is a stumbling block to mature faith.

Inadequate faith fails because it cannot deal maturely with the dark side of life. This faith does not have the inner resources to deal with adversity or tribulation. John 16 tried to prepare the church to face the difficult days. "They will put you out of the synagogues" (v. 2); they may kill you (v. 2); I am going to have to leave you, and you will have to do some grieving (v. 6). The record shows they did not listen.

One minister tells of being asked to preach in a church of one of the most famous television preachers today. On the way from the airport, the pulpit guest received these instructions: "People worship with us in order to feel good about themselves. . . . Don't mention the cross in your sermon. And don't dwell too much on sin."2 Shallow optimism will never produce a faith for the hard times.

Jesus asked this question to lead His disciples to a faith that would be adequate for whatever came.

Such a faith has few illusions. These believers see through a glass darkly. They know deep in their hearts that they can only know in part at best. These persons have learned the hard way that the way of faith is slippery at best. Even the most proficient of runners stumble and fall.

John Bunyan understood this concept of faith. He wrote of the pilgrims along the road who rejoiced in their progress and success. They thanked God that they were not like the others. Bunyan reminded his pilgrims that they were only at the midpoint in their journeys.

We all have a long way to go. There will be tests, rivers to cross, and enemies, inside and out. Christ warned His followers that the hour was coming when some of them would be scattered and alone. Real faith knows its vulnerabilities.

Adequate faith attempts to face reality. Peering through the mirror of the Gospel we see how far short we fall from the glory of God. We come to know that if we do make it, it will not be because we have arrived at some spiritual plateau. We find our way because in it all—thorns, crosses, blood, and tears—we are given God's great gift of peace.

Katherine Mansfield, the gifted author, died in 1922 at the age of thirty-four after a long struggle with illness. Besides her other writings, she left behind a journal in which she wrote:

I should like this to be accepted as my confession.

There is no limit to human suffering. When one thinks
"I have touched the bottom of the sea—now I can go no
deeper," one goes deeper . . .

I do not want to die without leaving a record of my
belief that suffering can be overcome. For I do believe
it. What must one do?

One must *submit.* Do not resist it. Take it. Be over-
whelmed. Accept it fully. Make it a *part of life.*

Everything in life that we really accept undergoes a
change. So suffering must become Love. . . . I must pass
from personal love to a greater love.[3]

Jesus told His disciples, "Truly, truly, I say to you, you
will weep and lament, but the world will rejoice; you
will be sorrowful, but your sorrow will turn into joy"
(16:20). Strong faith faces reality, and sorrow is transformed into joy.

Adequate faith endures because it is not alone. We
slip our hands in the Hand of God. Jesus reminded
those troubled disciples: I will send the Counselor to
you (v. 7). "He will guide you into all the truth" (v. 13).
"You have sorrow now, but I will see you again and your
hearts will rejoice" (v. 22). "I have said this to you, that
in me you may have peace" (v. 33).

The Christian is not immune to the difficulties of life.
Bad things *do* happen to good people. A house burns
down. A child dies. A father loses his job after twenty
years of faithfulness. A marriage fails. War breaks out in
a village in Nicaragua, and an innocent child is blinded
forever. Sickness disrupts our carefully made plans.
Life does not turn out as we thought.

But in John 16:32 we find His secret: "The hour is
coming, indeed it has come, when you will be scattered,
every man to his home, and will leave me alone; yet I

am not alone, for the Father is with me." Jesus placed His hands in the hands of the Father, and it was enough.

Jesus ended this whole chapter with words of reassurance: "I have said this to you, that in me you may have peace. In the world you have tribulation; but be of good cheer, I have overcome the world" (v. 33). Thomas Carlyle said he could not read these words without tears coming to his eyes. With the help of God, we take whatever comes. This is an adequate faith.

Years ago, I stood in a drugstore line waiting my turn to check out. In front of me were two women. One of the women turned to the other and said, "I don't know you, but I have been looking at you for years. I have always admired your hair. I love that pretty grey color. I'd give anything to have hair like yours. Can you tell me what you put on it. I think it is so pretty." There was a long pause. The other woman explained, "Honey I don't use anything on my hair at all. It turned this color almost overnight. We had a child to die suddenly. Then my husband took sick, lingered, and died. And I had some other troubles about that time. It just happened. My hair turned grey. You can't get this color out of a bottle."

Adequate faith knows there are some things that cannot be purchased at some counter. God comes to those hard places and dark times. He gives us the grace and strength to do whatever we must do. And what He gives is always enough. No wonder He asked the faith question so often.

Notes

1. Frederick Buechner, *The Magnificent Defeat* (New York: The Seabury Press, 1966), p. 42.

2. William H. Williamson, "Going Against the Stream," *The Christian Century*, 19-26 Dec. 1984, p. 1192.

3. *Journal of Katherine Mansfield*, ed. J. Middleton Murry (New York: Howard Fertig, 1974), p. 166-167.

17
The Suffering Question: John 18:1-11

If it weren't for the rocks in its bed, the stream would have no song.[1]
—Carl Perkins, on the ups and downs of his political career

There hung, for as long as I remember, a special painting in the little brick church where I grew up. The picture was a very good reproduction of Johann Heinrich Hoffman's "Christ in Gethsemane." The picture is familiar to us all. It has been reproduced in Bibles and in countless Sunday School leaflets. We saw the picture stamped on the back of those funeral home fans we cooled ourselves with on Sundays before air conditioning.

Every Sunday, the church bell would ring at five minutes until ten. I would make my way up First Avenue of the mill village where I lived, past the mill, walk two blocks to Fortieth Street. I would turn left, past the grade school, cross the street, climb the steps, walk through the tall white columns, turn left inside the vestibule, and enter the sanctuary. I slipped into the same pew Sunday after Sunday. Halfway back I sat down on the left side. Then I would look up, up above the pulpit and the choir into the face of Jesus.

In that painting, Jesus knelt in the garden. His hands were folded before Him on the rock in prayer. If you looked very close, in the distance you could make out the dim figures of the sleeping disciples. Further back, in the darkness, you could almost see the gates of the city of Jerusalem. It was night. The only light in the painting shone from above. The light illuminated the face of Jesus. It was the face that haunted that little boy, sitting there so well scrubbed in his starched white shirt, gazing up at the picture.

There were Sundays after church when I remember making my way up through the choir loft to stand close to the painting. I can even remember reaching out and touching the velvet it was painted on and marveling at its strange power. I remember being drawn to that picture again and again.

The garden portrayed so clearly in that painting is not as carefully defined in John's Gospel. John 18 begins the passion narrative by saying: "When Jesus had spoken these words, he went forth with his disciples across the Kidron valley, where there was a garden, which he and his disciples entered" (v. 1).

A great many events are compressed into one paragraph. Judas led the soldiers to arrest Jesus. Simon Peter, in anger and defiance, pulled out his sword and lopped off the ear of one enemy. Jesus strongly rebuked His disciple.

In this turbulent setting, Jesus asked the suffering question of Simon Peter. "Put your sword into its sheath; shall I not drink the cup which the Father has given me?" (v. 11). Only here does John use the word *cup.* Mark employs the word on several occasions to speak of Christ's suffering. This "cup" represented many things: Christ's pain, His agony at facing God's will of the cross. The "cup" was the facing of His own death.

Simon Peter had not understood at all. In an act of great courage, he had drawn his sword to protect His Lord. Simon would have spared his Lord that "cup."

Most of us do not want to face the suffering question either. We do not welcome suffering. We are more comfortable with growth, success, and acceptance.

Yet the picture of Christ in the garden remains. Gethsemane is at the heart of the story. Without that "cup" filled with suffering, pain, and death, there would have been no gospel.

The tools of Christ's trade reversed all the values the world holds important. The weapons of His warfare were never carnal. He chose the foolish things to confound the mighty. One day it would be a towel and a basin; another day it would be prayers and forgiveness. On another occasion it would be turning the other cheek and walking a second mile. There, at the end, He took a "cup" and drank all the hurt and pain the world could offer. The next two chapters of John's Gospel define more clearly the suffering question.

My own pilgrimage with the suffering of Jesus continued several years ago when I was invited back to that little church where I had grown up. It was an anniversary occasion, and they had invited people who had been members through the years to come back for that special day. As I prepared for that occasion, I remembered the painting that hung over the pulpit and the choir all my growing-up years. I had not thought of that picture in twenty years. But it all came back—the picture of Jesus in the garden. As we gathered that sunny morning, we shook hands, hugged one another, looked at one another's children, and remembered. As I stood to preach, I looked out on a sea of faces, and the memories washed over me. I talked to them that day about how we had lived all our lives while Jesus knelt in the garden.

I told them that once upon a time there had come One who knelt in a garden and prayed for the likes of us—One who took a "cup," terrible and bitter, and drank it all for us. And I told them that if He could endure and discover and find something redemptive in His journey, we could find it, too.

That morning, my old neighbors from down the street were there to see if I could preach. My mother had told me they both were dying of cancer. On the front row, there was the oldest member of the church and her husband and only daughter. Halfway back, on my right there was the sweetest woman I have even known: a widow with diabetes. After the service she came by to say that she could not see me, but she heard every word. She sat with her youngest, a seventeen-year-old boy on crutches.

In the balcony was a woman who had come all the way from Florida for the occasion. She had been divorced, but she had taught us faithfully in Training Union despite the whispers and the innuendos. Two rows from the back sat my old high school buddy, fat and bald as a billard ball. Beside him sat his wife, beautiful as the day we graduated but flawed with a fever that left her motor functions awry. A little old lady with grey hair was there on my far left. I remembered how she had told me one time that she had started working in the mill when she was nine years old. She had finally retired. She could neither read nor write, but she was there with a smile on her face.

On the front row was my neighbor. We had lived side by side, and I had played with her only son. She could not even hold a song book—the arthritis was so bad. She sat there, blinking back the tears, for she had lost her only son—my age—five years before with a heart ailment. We had all gathered to listen again to the old, old story. Jesus knelt in the garden and prayed for us all. And He took a "cup" and drank it for the suffering of us all.

No wonder, through the years, that little cotton-mill congregation kept that picture of Jesus in the garden high above their pulpit. It was a reminder that in it all—the good and the bad, the dark and the sunny— God identifies, God suffers, and God cares. The seventeenth question is the suffering question. It takes us all in. And, in the taking, it changes us one and all. For those who come to terms with the seventeenth question bear, believe, hope, and endure it all—not as the defeated—but more than conquerors.

Note

1. Linda Botts, *Loose Talk* (New York: Quick Fox/Rolling Stone Press, 1980), p. 85.

18
The Easter Question:
John 20:1-18

Any good Communications Expert would have told you
   it was a mistake.
If there's going to be a resurrection
It should be on a mountaintop
With saturation coverage, advance publicity,
A stand nearby to sell souvenirs,
And, up near the tomb, a special reserved section
   for the VIPs,
Roped off from the pushing, noisy, eager crowd.
You can't just walk out of death, come back to life
In an empty garden early on a Sabbath morning
When the world is sleeping in,
With only one weeping woman to exclaim "Rabboni!"
Any good Communications Expert would have told
   you:
If you do it that way, no one will ever know.[1]

                        —Joan Eheart Cinelli

Easter, in John's Gospel, is much like his Christmas
story. John 1 tells of no angels, stars, or shepherds. We
find no innkeepers or Wise Men or Herods. There was
only the simple pronouncement: "The Word became
flesh" (v. 14).

John's resurrection account is not as stark as his

Christmas story. But compared to the other Gospels, the stage is almost bare. His writing was understated and deliberate. As in the other Gospels, the risen Lord appeared only to the believers. But what we learn is that even the believers did not easily comprehend what was going on.

The agony of Calvary was finally over. The disciples had scattered. Judas was dead. Peter was numb with guilt and grief. John tried, as best he could, to care for Jesus' mother. Jesus' body had been placed in Joseph's borrowed tomb. The Roman soldiers had sealed the door.

Black Saturday, the sabbath, must have come and gone as a blur. Travel was not permitted on that holy day. But early the next morning, Mary of Magdala had made her way to the tomb. Long ago, Jesus had cast out her seven devils. He had given her back her dignity by inviting her into His new family.

But that morning when she arrived at the tomb, she did not linger long. The guards were gone. The door was open. She was afraid. She had run and told Simon and John what she had seen. They came to reckon with the wonder of Easter morning. They left, exuberant and singing, but Mary must have missed them. John wrote that she made her way back to the tomb where she wept. Through the tears of her own grief, she made out a figure she presumed was the gardener. With infinite tenderness, He had called her name, and she knew who He was. It was the beginning of a story as unlikely as any story could be. She had seen her Lord, and she could not tell of this miracle fast enough or often enough. There would be many more encounters between the risen Christ and defeated disciples, but John tells us that Mary is remembered because she was the first one to meet Him face-to-face on Easter morning.

Could there be a more unusual Easter beginning? The tomb was empty, and Mary wept. She wept for many reasons. The One who had changed her life was dead and gone. She wept as she remembered the Cross. She had been there with Jesus' mother and John and the other Mary. She had seen it all. No wonder she wept. She wept because on that Sunday morning, someone had come and stolen the body of Jesus.

All this is the setting of the Easter question. Jesus spoke to Mary: "Woman, why are you weeping? Whom do you seek?" (v. 15). She thought He was the gardener. She could not see Him because her heart was filled with grief, and her eyes were blinded by tears. "Sir, if you have carried him away, tell me where you have laid him, and I will take him away" (v. 15).

Jesus then called her name. Mary, for the first time, recognized His voice. She called Him: "Teacher!" (v. 16). She knew who He was. She wiped away her tears and went to tell the disciples: "I have seen the Lord" (v. 18). A prominent New Testament scholar, C. K. Barrett, has said that this paragraph is John's main statement on the resurrection.[2]

What does this Easter question mean? The risen Christ comes to us where we are. The last thing Mary expected was to see Jesus. Too much had happened— the Cross had been indelibly stamped on her memory. The best she had ever known had been nailed to a cross. It was all unjust, unfair, and rigged. Jesus had done no harm. How wrong it all was! No wonder she wept. She wept for Jesus, for herself. She may have wept for them all.

John's story says that Easter comes to us where we are. We do not even have to recognize His presence or know who He is. That's the incredible part. God comes to us wherever we are.

What was Jesus' response to the weeping Mary? He did not say: "You shouldn't cry. It's Easter. Rejoice! Listen to the trumpets. A new day has come." No. Christ stood there in the shadows asking her about her tears. "Why are you weeping?"

He meets us where we are: Thomas with his doubts, Peter in his shame, Mary with a heart so heavy she thought she would die. Jesus first appeared after His resurrection to a woman who wept. Easter, then, meets us where we are. And Easter is big enough for all the conditions of life.

Holidays, like Easter, are hard for folk who have known tragedy. They have little to celebrate. They feel numb on the inside. They fear going out in public. They find themselves losing control in the strangest times. So they stay away from church, especially on the special days. Some are separated. Some are going through a very trying divorce. Sometimes they have lost a loved one in death. Sometimes there is a child in trouble, a business that has failed, or depression that has immobolized them. Easter with its lilies and trumpets means little to them.

John's Gospel says that Easter comes to us where we are. Our pain is not brushed aside by the hosannas and the grandeur of the resurrection. The real Easter asks about tears, aches, and blind eyes that see nothing clearly. "Why are you weeping?" is not just another question. It is *the* Easter question.

Mary did not know who spoke to her. She thought it

was the gardener. But suddenly, all the pieces fell into place. Her name was called: "Mary" (v. 16). She recognized Jesus' voice. She had first heard it years before when Jesus called out the seven devils from her troubled, tortured life. She had heard it in Bethany when Jesus had said: "Lazarus, come forth" (11:43, KJV). She had heard that voice from a cross. Mary answered: "Rab-boni!" *My Teacher!* [3] She knew who called her name.

Easter, then, is a personal message. Our names are called. We are addressed. Samuel Shoemaker understood this well. He was one of the great Episcopal ministers of this century. He wrote many books, helped found Alcoholics Anonymous, and the faith and work movement. His evangelistic ministry was known around the world. Such a busy man had little time at home, but he was very devoted to his family. When his little girl, Sally, was two and a half, Dr. Shoemaker decided she was old enough to join her parents in their prayer time. The father and mother would kneel by the crib, and Dr. Shoemaker would tell Sally that if she was very quiet Jesus would come and put His thoughts into her mind. One night she bowed her head and folded her hands. In a short time, she popped her head up, and her eyes were shining bright. Her father asked her, "Sally Falls, did Jesus say anything to you?" Sally replied, "Yes, Daddy, He said 'Sally Falls.' He knowed my name." [4]

Easter is the recognition that He knows our names, and we are called. "My Sheep hear my voice, and I know them, and they follow me" (10:27).

He who knows our names evokes a great response. Moses, long ago, found forgiveness that day his name was called. Samuel found his life's work as a priest. Isaiah, crying in the Temple, found his role as a prophet defined. Nicodemus discovered new life in his middle years. Nathanael discovered the meaning of life when his name was called. And a very troubled woman with seven terrible devils met One who gave her back a wholeness. When our names are called and we make our response, Easter always brings new life.

Mary returned to tell the disciples that she had seen the risen Lord. The picture that she then carried of her Lord was not broken and flyspecked on Calvary—defeated and dead. She carried a different picture. The risen Lord was triumphant and alive. Mary's days were lived out in the light of this incredible truth.

A man visited the Grand Canyon for the first time. As he stood looking over the vistas, the colors, and the wonder, he stood in silence. Suddenly he exclaimed, "My, something must have happened here!" Such a vast chasm was too big and awe-inspiring for words or explanations. Such was the early church's response to Easter: Something happened there.

What photograph of Jesus do we carry with us? Is it some cracked and yellowing picture of someone who died on a cross two thousand years ago? Or, like Mary, is it a picture of the risen Lord, large enough for all we face?

Mary slipped from the stage and was scarcely heard from again. But she was the first witness to the risen Lord. She was the recipient of the Easter question. It came to her one day when her world was blurred and blinded by the tears of so much grief. But He addressed her weeping and called her name. Her life was changed forever.

Notes

1. Joan Eheart Cinelli, from unpublished poem used by permission of the author.

2. C. K. Barrett, *The Gospel According to Saint John* (London: S.P.C.K., 1958), p. 466.

3. A. T. Robertson, *Word Pictures in the New Testament,* vol. 5 (Nashville: Sunday School Board of the SBC, 1932), p. 312.

4. Helen Smith Shoemaker, *I Stand by the Door* (Harper & Row, 1967), p. 71.

19
The Belief Question:
John 20:19-29

What we are in desperate need of today is for people who have more than a secondhand acquaintance with God—who have discovered a faith of their own.

We shall find it, as have the Thomases . . ." *a faith of our own.* If we are honest and struggle with the questions, if we are open and flexible, the light shall come and we shall see.[1]

—Roger Lovette

Jesus raised two questions in John 20. He first asked Mary why she wept. He returned to the theme which runs throughout this book. In another faith question, Jesus asked Thomas: "Have you believed because you have seen me? Blessed are those who have not seen and yet believe" (v. 29).

We have already learned that belief and faith are important words in this Gospel. Early in His ministry, Jesus asked the would-be disciple Nathanael why he believed. Underneath His conversation with Nicodemus, He really talked about faith and trust. More than once He turned to the crowd and asked if they believed. He asked Martha and the disciples about their own belief. John summarized the intention of his Gospel at the end of chapter 20 by writing: "But these are written that you may believe that Jesus is the Christ, the Son of God, and that believing you may have life in his name" (v. 31).

The belief question is answered in this Gospel in a variety of ways. Faith means many things and evokes a multitude of responses.

John's resurrection account makes this very clear. Early that morning, Peter and another disciple discovered the empty tomb. They returned to their homes excited and breathless. There is a faith that needs little evidence: it simply believes.

That story is followed by Mary's experience. On Easter morning she could not hold back her tears because the tomb was empty. She believed only when the Lord called her name, then she saw Him.

Jesus then appeared to the troubled disciples behind closed doors. They were afraid, and Jesus came to them, showing them the stab wounds and the scars. They saw Him and knew He was alive.

Thomas was not present on that occasion. When he heard their report of Jesus' Easter visit, he could not believe: "Unless I see in his hands the print of the nails, and place my finger in the mark of the nails, and place my hand in his side, I will not believe" (v. 25). Eight days later they gathered again, and this time Thomas was there. The Lord came and showed Thomas the nailprints in His hands. This doubting disciple made a great confession: "My Lord and my God!" (v. 28).

For years, the church has been too hard on Thomas. We have talked about the doubter as if there was something very wrong in his response. Thomas only asked to see what his friends had seen.

We learn from these four different resurrection appearances that God uses a multitude of ways to evoke a faith response from His people. No one experience is normative for us all. Each separate encounter was valid and real.

Madeleine L'Engle understood this truth when she wrote:

> I happen to love spinach, but my husband, Hugh, does not; he prefers beets, which I don't much care for—except the greens. Neither of us thinks less of the other because of this difference in taste. But spinach and beets are vegetables; both are good for us. We do not have to enjoy precisely the same form of balanced meal.
>
> We approach God in rather different ways, but it is the same God we are seeking.[2]

As we make our own response, Christ meets our separate needs. Once in a Vacation Bible School class, I asked the children in my group which child they felt their parents loved best. Three children from the same family raised their hands. Each one said they thought their mother loved them the best. She had done such a good job of parenting that she made each of her children think they were quite special.

Thomas had to see for himself. God came to him. Mary needed a special word, and Jesus called her name. Huddled behind locked doors, those disciples needed some sense of God's presence, and He provided what they needed. Those two that first discovered the empty tomb needed no more proof than the knowledge that Jesus was not there. All four separate encounters were valid faith experiences.

God in Jesus Christ meets our individual needs one

by one. As the Shepherd calls each sheep by name, He knows the needs that are unique to us alone.

One pastor was invited to eat the evening meal with a family in his church. As he stopped his car and walked up the sidewalk, he was met with two boys, ages seven and five. The five-year-old was retarded. As they walked to the house, their father drove up into the driveway. Both boys left the preacher and ran to their daddy. On the way, the seven-year-old stopped and picked up a flower to present to his father. The retarded son did not quite understand. He reached down, picked up a handful of dust and rocks to give to his father. The dad picked each boy up and hugged him. The preacher heard the father say, "Thank you for the flower. And thank *you* for the rocks."

As God dealt with Thomas's needs, so He will deal with us all. And in our own experiences, we can come to say: "My Lord and my God!" We finally learn what each disciple learned, to say our confession in our way and in our own account.

Faith wears many faces, and if we respond to Him we can all be taken in. When John wrote, most of the eye-witnesses had either died or had been killed. One of the concerns of those who had only heard the story was that their experiences could never measure up to those who had walked with Him in Galilee.

This last faith question shatters that argument once and for all: "Have you believed because you have seen me? Blessed are those who have not seen and yet believe" (v. 29).

Notes

1. Roger Lovette, *A Faith of Our Own* (Philadelphia: Pilgrim Press, 1976), p. 135.

2. Madeline L'Engle. Reprinted from *Walking on Water, Reflections on Faith and Art* by permission of Harold Shaw Publishers, copyright © Crosswicks, 1980, p. 45.

20
The Love Question:
John 21:15-19

"Love is not a feeling. It is a person."[1]
—Madeleine L'Engle

Easter had come and gone. The dust had settled. The disciples had scattered. They were wrung out emotionally. Too much had happened too fast. It was as if all the colors had run together, and they couldn't sort them out. It seemed like a million years since that upper room. There had been the bread and the wine, in the middle of it all an apron, towel, and water. Christ had prayed in a garden, Judas had come with the soldiers, and Simon had tried to defend Him with a sword. But it had done no good. The soldiers had dragged Him away. Peter had cursed and denied Him that very night. Then came the trial and the scourging when His back was beaten to a pulp, and they had been so afraid.

Then as if that was not enough, there came black Friday, the weeping women, and the brokenhearted John. Calvary was so awful with its dried blood and flies, armed guards, and finally Joseph's dark tomb. Saturday was the longest day they had ever spent. But, finally, it gave way to Easter. And what a day that had been! Breathless women, sunrise, a stone rolled away, a door opened, and a gardener turned angel. It was all more than they could understand. So the colors just ran together. It took a genius named John to sort it all out years later, the bits and the pieces, the emotions, the facts, and the poetry of that terribly real and promising story.

Jesus' twentieth question was spoken a short time after Easter. The words are found in John's last chapter. Those first believers did not meet to celebrate, praise, or do anything that we would think appropriate for that Easter occasion. Their response seemed inappropriate at best. They huddled together in the shadows. They tried to sort out all that had happened and make sense of the whole business they had been through.

This is as modern a story as we have in the Bible. Easter had come and gone, and Simon Peter did not know what to do. Finally, John said, the fisherman returned to his nets. What was a man to do? One could not sit around holding hands and singing all the time. The other disciples trailed behind Peter.

They fished all night and caught nothing. Toward morning a voice called from the misty shore, "How many did you catch?" "Not many," they said, which any fisherman knew was probably their way of saying they had not caught a single fish. The voice responded, "Cast your nets over on the other side." When they did, their nets were filled to capacity. John, peering through the mist, recognized the figure on the seashore. "It is the Lord." Peter, because he was a good swimmer, jumped into the water and made his way to shore. Christ had fixed breakfast. And this became the setting of what we call the love question. It was addressed to Peter.

We can all breathe a sigh of relief that these words

were spoken to Peter. If He came to Peter with a face like his and a temperament like his, He can come to any of us. Peter was impulsive and emotional. He was dogmatic and always right. Peter was stubborn, strong, hardworking, and opinionated. More than all of these— he was a disciple who had failed. "I will never leave you," he had bragged. Yet before the night had ended, he had cursed and railed out before the fire: "I do not know the man" (Matt. 26:74). Deep in his heart he knew that he had failed the best, the loveliest, the purest One he had ever known. After that, the Scriptures say, he wept bitterly as a cock crowed somewhere in the distance.

Later, he hid with the others. They were all afraid for their own skins. And even after seeing the resurrected Lord on Easter, it wasn't enough. Peter unrolled his nets and went back to the only thing he was sure of. Even that didn't work. He and his friends fished all night and nothing happened.

Jesus' question by the seashore turned Peter inside out. Despite his failures, Jesus took him aside. And if this be true, despite our betrayals He comes to us, too. He comes as He came to Simon Peter—after our temptations, impatience, and misdeeds.

Peter could not look him in the eye. He kept trying to clear his throat because his voice sounded so hoarse. There was a lump in his throat. Jesus and Peter, off to one side of the stage, whispering so the others could not hear. If Jesus came to Simon Peter after all his sins, He will come to us, too.

What did Jesus say? "Simon, son of John, do you love me more than these?" (v. 15). Their eyes met. The question was: "Do you love Me? Do you love Me more than these?" This was a terrible question. Jesus asked it over and over again.

Simon answered: "You know" (v. 15). Lord, You know the truth. Twice he said the same thing. "You know," (v. 16). You see. You know everything. You recognize the truth when it is spoken. You know the facts: my name and address and family. You know all the details of my life. Lord, these You recognize. You know that I do love you.

But the third time Simon responded, he changed the word from the ordinary *Lord, You know* to another word. This other knowing in the Greek is a different word entirely (v. 17). You see it all. Down below the surface, underneath my betrayals and my cowardly denials—You know. You really *know* me.

Easter celebrates the incredible truth of this second knowing. There is One who knows us through and through, and sees deep down below the surface. God knows, we say. Indeed He does.

What was Jesus' response? He gave Simon a commission: "Feed my lambs. . . . Tend my sheep. . . . Feed my sheep" (vv. 15-17). If you really love Me, you've got to do something. Begin with the little ones, and supply whatever needs they have. Next, shepherd the flock. This was harder. You must exercise more responsibility. Guide the sheep. And then: Feed the sheep which was the hardest demand of them all. For the stubborn old sheep covered with cockleburs would not listen to anything. They were hardheaded, rebellious. They all had needs. Feed My sheep.

What Jesus really meant is that if you really do love Me—Peter, James, Joe, or Roger—you will let that love flow out to all the others—first to the lambs, the little ones, the children. But this love doesn't stop there. Feed My sheep, and then even the old, ornery, and difficult ones until the whole world is included. Feed them all.

Peter must have answered in the affirmative. After that chilly morning, Simon was a changed man. He was strong, powerful, and authoritative (see Acts 2). People listened to him. He became one of the key leaders in the early church. Acts says that his shadow fell on people's lives, and they were healed (3:12-16). He preached, and thousands responded. The disciple who failed became the disciple who could be counted on.

Jesus came quiet as the morning mist—over breakfast. Peter had fished all night and caught nothing. He was ashamed of so many things in his life. There were broken promises and words he could not keep. Jesus came—asking the broken, embarrassed disciple if he loved Him. And, in a feeble, halting kind of way he nodded and finally said, "You know." The old betrayer was given a charge. Go out and do what you must do— what you were destined to do the day you were born. And Simon Peter reached up and claimed his heritage.

Note

1. Madeline L'Engle, *A Circle of Quiet* (New York: The Seabury Press, 1979), p. 45.

21
The Final Question:
John 21:20-23

God becomes a reality to us when He lays upon us a commission.[1]

—John Oxenham

The story is almost over. The props have all been taken away from the stage. The crosses have been hauled away. The empty tomb is nowhere in sight. The little boy with his loaves and fishes, the crippled man with his pallet, the blind man with his tin cup have all slipped away. The crowds are no more. Even the Pharisees and the Sanhedrin have vanished.

John ended as he had begun—by the seashore. Again, it was morning. Breakfast was over and done with. The sun came up over the hills, ushering in a new day. It was time to go back to work. One last question remained.

Peter, of course, prompted it. One would think that after Peter's graceful encounter after breakfast he would have remained silent. But the old Simon intruded once more. Pointing to another disciple, he asked: "Lord, what about this man?" (v. 21). Jesus must have smiled: "If it is my will that he remain until I come, what is that to you? Follow me!" (v. 22).

The ten remaining disciples must have overheard

that question of responsibility: "What is that to you?" They also must have heard Jesus' challenge: *Peter, your discipleship is not to be confused with another's. Each disciple is different, and each task I give is personal. Comparisons and contrasts have no place in My Kingdom. Peter, you are to follow, John is to follow, and all the others are to follow.*

The church that first heard John's words faced a terrible crisis in spirit. They did not know if they could hang on. So much in their world was harsh, unkind, cruel, and unfair. They longed for the old days. If only they could have been there like Peter, John, or even Mary in the garden. How different it all would have been!

John wrote that none of that mattered. Each age must take up its own tasks and follow its own voices. They could not fret about all the others who had lived when Christ was on earth. They could only follow Him down whatever roads that lay out before them.

Follow Me, Jesus says. Through good days and bad. Follow Me through it all. Give yourself with abandon, love, allegiance, and even courage.

The last question, out of all the crowded questions, may be the best question. We are only responsible for what we do and what we have been given. The rest is left to God.

Follow Me!

Note

1. John Oxenham, *I Quote,* ed. Virginia Ely (Westwood, N. J.: Fleming H. Revell Co., 1947), p. 294.

MEPKIN ABBEY
1098 Mepkin Abbey Road
Moncks Corner, S.C. 29461